The Book of Compassion
Reverence for All Life

(A Collection of Articles)

Compiled by

Pramoda Chitrabhanu

Jain Meditation International Center
P.O.Box 230244 Ansonia
New York, NY 10023-0244

Telephone: (212) 362-6483
E-mail : pramodac@hotmail.com
Website – www.jainmeditation.org

Pravin K. Shah

Jain Study Center of North Carolina
509 Carriage Woods Circle
Raleigh, NC 27607-3969 USA

Telephone: (919) 859-4994
E-mail: education@jaina.org
Website – www.jaina.org

1

The Book of Compassion - JES 921
(JAINA Education Series 921 - Reference Book)
Fourth Edition : February 2006
ISBN : 1-59406-042-8

This book has no copyright

Use the religious material respectfully

Please provide us with your comments and suggestions.

Support JAINA Education activities.
Your contribution is tax deductible in USA.

Published and Distributed by :
Federation of Jain Associations in North America

JAINA Education Committee
Pravin K. Shah, Chairperson
509 Carriage Woods Circle
Raleigh, NC 27607-3969 USA
Telephone and Fax - 919-859-4994
Email - education@jaina.org
Websites - www.jaina.org

Use the above address for communication and for availability of the Education books in other countries

The Book is also available from the following Organizations :

**Jain Meditation
International Center**
P.O. Box 230244 Ansonia
New York, NY 10023-0244 USA

Telephone – 212-362-6483
E-mail – jainmamata@aol.com
Website - www.jainmeditation.org

**Jain Study Center of
North Carolina**
509 Carriage Woods Circle
Raleigh, NC 27607-3969 USA

Telephone – 919-859-4994
E-mail – education@jaina.org
Website – www.jaina.org

Printed by : Amrut Printers, India.

DEDICATED

To

Acharya Shri Hemchandracharya

શ્રી હેમચંદ્રાચાર્ય   રાજા કુમારપાળ

(1089 AD to1173 AD)

Acharya Shri Hemchandracharya's life was a living example of compassion and love. During his life he touched the lives of many and one of them was King Kumarpal of Gujarat. His teaching of Ahimsa and compassion towards all living beings was a turning point in the life of the king. He came to understand that by the power of refusing to harm any living creature, one could gather strength to dispel much pain and suffering from the face of the earth.

Acharya Shree Hemchandracharya convinced the king to issue an order to all his people to stop animal torturing or killing for food, sport or fun. Thus for many generations the State of Gujarat became vegetarian and no one engaged in any kind of animal killing or torturing.

This is a most unusual and hopeful incident for mankind that for a certain period in its history a whole state came to observe the ancient principle of Ahimsa.

'The purpose of living beings is to assist each other.'

Tattvarth-Sutra (Chapter 5, Sutra 21)

Table of Contents

A Few Words

Many times we write because we are urged from within to open our feelings on paper and share them with others. This book came into existence as a result of our strong feeling for the subject and thus writing was a natural consquence of the passion we felt.

Non-violence (Ahimsa) is the highest principle of the religions of the East. In Padma puran (1:31:27) it is said, "Ahimsa Parmo Dharma" meaning Non-violence is the highest duty. These way eastern religions have taught the principle of compassion to the people and they have traditionally revered animals. Most of them do not take meat, fish, eggs, and alcohol and their concern for animals goes beyond vegetarianism. Their scriptures demonstrate deep reverences and love for them. Animal symbols and stories pervade their tradition. For centuries, specifically Jains have protected and cared for animals by establishing many animal and bird sanctuaries (panjarapoles) and hospitals in India.

However, recent technological advances have created a new environment for violence not visible to common people. The use and abuse of animals raised for slaughter far exceeds our imagination. The cruelty to dairy cows and other animals has reached its peak behind the walls of dairy farms and slaughter houses. Their owners, both industries and associated people treat animals and birds (chickens etc.) as commodities. Animals are produced on a large scale through artificial insemination and other means. The owners exploit and torture these animals on a large scale during the prime of their life and ultimately slaughter them well before the end of their natural life spans.

Even though most of the people of India are vegetarians the use of dairy products, wearing of silk and wool clothes still continues. Also the animal byproducts that are used in cookies, candy, clothing, footwear, household cleaning supplies, cosmetics, medicines, and in performing religious rituals are used by them on a daily basis.

The purpose of this book is to educate readers and other concerned and compassionate people regarding the high tech cruelty to all types of animals that exists in the production of dairy, silk, wool, and other products. By reading the various articles, you will realize that cruelty to animals occurs, in a similar way, in the USA, India, in big cities, villages, and the world at large.

By consuming dairy (milk, cheese, butter, ghee, ice-cream) and other products as mentioned above we directly support large-scale cruelty to animals. One should pay attention to animals, not in a sentimental way, but in a way that gives both animals and humans the freedom to pursue their own paths and to fulfill their self-made destinies.

It is our humble request to the readers that they should try to reduce the use of dairy products, silk, wool, and varakh at home and in temples and in rituals. Also they should serve vegan (vegetarian food without dairy products) food in religious function

The information on various articles were collected from many sources over many years. In particular, we have collected significant information from People for the Ethical Treatment of Animals (PETA *Ingrid Newkirk*), *Beauty Without Cruelty (India), Dr. Neal D. Bernard's* books and tapes, the literature and articles of *John Robbins, Dr. Dean Ornish, Dr. Narendra Sheth, Sangeeta Kumar* and *Dr. Christopher Chapel.* We are very thankful for their contributions and for the contributions of many others in the fields of non-violence, ecology, compassion and the environment.

We are highly obliged to *Gurudev Shri Chitrabhanuji* who has been a constant encouragement to us in compiling and publishing this book.

We hope this booklet will be well-received by its readers and will serve its intended purpose of educating them. If you have any more information, comments, or corrections to the information found in any of the articles, please let us know. We continuously update these articles and add new information.

Pramoda Chitrabhanu

Jain Meditation International Center, New York

Pravin K. Shah

Jain Study Center of North Carolina (Raleigh)

UNIVERSAL DECLARATION OF THE RIGHTS OF ANIMALS

Final text adopted by the International League for Animal Rights and affiliated national leagues on the occasion of the Third International Meeting on the Rights of Animals (London 21-23 September, 1977). The Declaration, proclaimed on 15 October 1978 by the International League, affiliated leagues, associations and individuals who wish to be associated with it, will be submitted to the United Nations Educational, Scientific and Cultural Organization (UNESCO), and then to the United Nations Organization (UNO).

PREAMBLE

Whereas all animals have rights;

Whereas disregard and contempt for the rights of animals has resulted and continues to result in crimes by man against nature and against animals;

Whereas recognition by the human species of the right to existence of other animal species is the foundation of the co-existence of species throughout the animal world;

Whereas genocide has been perpetrated by man on animals and the threat of genocide continues;

Whereas respect for animals is linked to the respect of man for men;

Whereas, from childhood, man should be taught to observe, understand, respect and love animals;

IT IS HEREBY PROCLAIMED:

Article 1

All animals are born with an equal claim on life and the same rights to existence.

Article 2

* All animals are entitled to respect.
* Man as an animal species shall not arrogate to himself the right to exterminate or inhumanely exploit other animals. It is his duty to use his knowledge for the welfare of animals.
* All animals have the right to the attention, care and protection of man.

Article 3

* No animal shall be ill-treated or shall be subject to cruel acts.
* If an animal has to be killed, this must be instantaneous and with out distress.

Article 4

* All wild animals have the right to liberty in their natural environment, whether land, air or water, and should be allowed to procreate.
* Deprivation of freedom, even for educational purposes, is an in fringement of this right.

Article 5

* Animals of species living traditionally in a human environment have the right to live and grow at the rhythm and under the conditions of life and freedom peculiar to their species.
* Any interference by man with this rhythm or these conditions for purposes of gain is an infringement of this right.

Article 6

* All companion animals have the right to complete their natural life span.
* Abandonment of an animal is a cruel and degrading act.

Article 7

All working animals are entitled to a reasonable limitation of the duration and intensity of their work, to necessary nourishment, and to rest.

Article 8

- Animal experimentation involving physical or psychological suf fering is incompatible with the rights of animals whether it be for scientific, medical, commercial, or any other form of research.
- Replacement methods must be used and developed.

Article 9

Where animals are used in the food industry, they shall be reared, transported, lairaged and killed without the infliction of suffering.

Article 10

- No animal shall be exploited for the amusement of man.
- Exhibitions and spectacles involving animals are incompat ible with their dignity.

Article 11

Any act involving the wanton killing of an animal is biocide, that is, a crime against life.

Article 12

- Any act involving mass killing of wild animals is genocide, that is, a crime against the species.
- Pollution or destruction of the natural environment leads to genocide.

Article 13

- Dead animals shall be treated with respect.
- Scenes of violence involving animals shall be banned from cinema and television, except for humane education.

Article 14

- Representatives of movements that defend animal rights should have an effective voice at all levels of government.
- The rights of animals, like human rights, should enjoy the protection of law.

Pravin K. Shah
Jain Study Center of North Carolina (Raleigh)

My Visit to A Dairy Farm

A Dairy Visit in the USA:

I visited a dairy farm with about 150 cows located on Route 2 north of Burlington, Vermont (USA) in May of 1995. All of its milk production is used to make ice cream. Here is what I saw and learned:

- The cows are machine-milked for 3.5 minutes each. This is done without regard to how hard it is on the cow. It was extremely difficult to watch the cows suffer during milking. The machine has no feeling and, to extract the last drop of milk, sometimes traces of blood get mixed with the milk.

- Every morning, hormones or drugs are injected into the cows to increase their milk yield. They are also fed a diet geared toward high production of milk. The dairy cow produces 20 times the amount of milk a cow on the traditional family farm produces.

- Since cows produce the most milk after pregnancy, they are kept continuously pregnant through artificial insemination.

- The gestation period of a cow is 9 months; the same as for humans. If a male calf, of no use to the dairy industry, is born, he is shipped to the veal industry within two or three days of birth. The evening I was there, the farm was shipping three baby calves in a truck to a veal factory. The mother cows were crying when their babies were separated from them. I cannot forget the scene and can still hear the cries of the mother cows.

- The veal industry is the most cruel meat industry in the world. It produces very tender meat that is considered a delicacy. The baby calves are raised in darkness in a very confining crate, which allows practically no movement. They are fed an iron deficient diet to make their flesh tender and properly textured. They are slaughtered at six months. There is much literature available about cruelty in the veal industry.

- Within two months of delivery, the cows are impregnated again. I did not have the stamina to watch the process of artificial insemination that the farm was showing off.

- About four to five times a year, this farm would take the cows outside for a walk. Otherwise, the cows are tied in one place and they have no choice but to defecate where they are confined. It stunk badly when I was there; the farm would wash the confinement areas once or twice a day, and the remaining times the cows would live in their own waste.

- The life expectancy of a cow is about 15 years. However, after about 4 to 5 years, their milk production capacity drops significantly so these cows are sent to the slaughterhouse for cheap meat which is used in fast food restaurants, for hot dog filler, dog and cat food, and a variety of other "foodstuffs". The rest of the body material (by-products) turns up in products like floor wax, pet food, medicines, insulin, gelatin, footwear, upholstery, taco fillings, cosmetics, candles, and soaps.

- During her fertile life, a cow delivers about four babies. Statistically, only one female baby is needed to replace the existing cow. Hence all other babies (males or females) are sent to the veal industry where they are tortured for six months and then slaughtered for their meat (delicacy meal).

As I learned and observed the cruelty in the dairy industry, I at first found it hard to believe. On a personal level, I feared that it would be impossible for me to give up dairy products and become vegan (absolutely no animal products). How could I eliminate milk, yogurt, butter, ghee, and cheese from my diet? To become vegan means that I cannot drink tea with milk, eat any Indian sweets, pizza, milk chocolate, Ice cream, eggless but dairy-containing cake, and many other items.

At this time I remembered my daughter Shilpa's (who became vegan a few months prior to my visit) words, *"Dad, cows' milk is for baby cows and not for humans or their babies. No other animal consumes the milk of another species. We do not have the right to consume the milk of other animals for our benefit by exploiting and torturing them. Furthermore, milk and its products are not essential for our survival or for healthy life".*

Needless to say, the dairy farm tour made me an instan vegan.

A Dairy Visit in India

In November of 1995, I also visited a dairy farm near Mumbai in India. I observed similar things. Overall, things were actually worse because there are few enforced regulations. During my visits to

India in 1997 and 1998, I learned more about Indian dairy operations.

Many dairies in India do not own cows. Milk is supplied to the dairy industry by local cowherds who own the cows. The local cowherds generally own 10 to 40 cows and they do not use machines to milk the cows.

However, they keep cows pregnant all the time for a continuous supply of milk. Every year each cow delivers a baby. The local cowherds can not absorb all the baby calves that are born every year in their business. Hence, they sell the baby calves (70 to 80% of them) to the beef industry where the calves are raised for beef and are slaughtered in three to four years, or to an illegal veal industry where they are slaughtered in six months. In the holy city of Palitana, I found a newly born calf lying dead in a field close to my cousin's home. After investigation I found that a cow had delivered a baby calf in the field and the owner just left the newly born calf in the field to die and carried the mother cow back to his place.

After four to five deliveries, the milk yield of an adult cow drops significantly and hence the cowherd replaces the old cow with a young one and sells the old cow to a slaughterhouse for cheap meat. Only a few cows (5% or less) end up in a cow shelter called Panjarapole.

In comparison, it seems the maximum cruelty lies in the following actions which are the same in India, the USA and the rest of world:

- Keeping the cows continuously pregnant and continuously milked during pregnancy.

- Slaughtering 70% to 80% of calves within six months by the veal industry, or within five years by the beef industry; or allowing the calf to die just after birth.

- Slaughtering the mother cows after five years of their fertile life even though their life expectancy is 15 to 20 years.

Organic Milk:

The Organic dairy farm is generally smaller than the huge factory-style farm. Organic milk is produced without the use of antibiotics, pesticides, and hormones. Milk additives are not used.

However to ensure steady milk production, *the organic dairy farms:*

- Keep cows pregnant all the time through artificial insemination or other means

- Continuosly milked during pregnancy.

- Sell baby calves to the veal or beef industry where they are slaughtered in six months to five years

- Sell the adult cows to the slaughterhouses after four years when the milk production yield drops.

Also there are no legal regulations that prevent dairy farmers from engaging in similar abuses such as keeping the cows in tie stalls, using electric milking equipment, etc. Few organic farms treat cows properly during their milk-producing life.

Hence organic milk is not cruelty-free milk.

American Slaughterhouse Statistics:

The New York Times reported on May 12, 1996 that on an average day the following numbers of animals are slaughtered in American slaughterhouses.

ANIMALS/BIRDS	NUMBER KILLED PER DAY IN USA
Cattle	130,000
Calves	7,000
Hogs	360,000
Chickens	24,000,000

Please let me know if you have similar statistics for India.

HEALTH ISSUES

After becoming vegan, I have researched health related issues and summarized my findings as follows:

Calcium and Protein

Most Americans consume two to three times more protein from animal source (milk, cheese, and meat) than their daily requirements. Many scientific studies show that the people who consume an animal based, high protein diet have lots of calcium in their urine but vegetarians do not.

The protein in animal products (such as milk, cheese or meat) is more acidic than vegetable protein. The body neutralizes extra acid associated with animal protein by drawing calcium from bones. This causes calcium deficiency in the bones causing diseases like osteoporosis for the people who consume dairy or meat products. Also their kidneys have to work harder to remove the waste of calcium that leached from bones to blood. The net result is that the people who consume animal base high protein diet lose the calcium from their bones and their kidneys are more susceptible to fail.

Vegetarians get enough protein from their diet but not an excessive amount. Vegetable protein is less acidic than animal protein hence it does not leach calcium from the bones. The calcium absorbed by consuming dark green vegetables and various other vegetarian sources is maintained by the bones at a much healthier rate. The end result is that vegetarians who get their calcium from non-animal sources, such as dark green vegetables, develop stronger bones, not weaker ones and calcium is not found in their urine. Much scientific evidence indicates that milk is not essential for strong bones.

However one should remember that thinning of the bones occur among older people regardless they consume the milk or not. This problem is more severe among the older people who use more dairy and other animal products. This is due to the protein effect (large amount of protein in diet and calcium is leached out) as indicated above. Postmenopausal women are particularly at risk for osteoporosis. Milk does not seem to protect the bones of older people.

In conclusion, vegetarians get enough calcium and protein as long as they eat a good variety of plant foods to maintain their natural weight. They are less susceptible to osteoporosis and kidney failure.

Cholesterol

Cholesterol is a material similar to wax. It makes hormones and other elements for our body. Only the liver of animal and human bodies makes cholesterol. Hence, externally cholesterol is found only in animal products such as meat, milk, cheese and other dairy and nonvegeterian food. A pure vegetarian diet (fruits, vegetables, grains, and lentils) has no cholesterol.

Generally the liver of human produces cholesterol in sufficient quantities for its bodily needs. However, when we consume dairy or meat products, we also consume animal cholesterol. In this way we accumulate excess cholesterol. This excess cholesterol in the body is harmful because it gets deposited in our arteries. Ultimately, clogged arteries result in heart attacks.

Saturated and Unsaturated Fat

Saturated fat aggravates the liver to produce more cholesterol than the body normally requires. Almost all animal fats, butter (ghee), and some vegetable oils (coconut, palm etc.) are saturated fat. Some vegetarians have high cholesterol due to the high content of satu-rated fat in their diet. One should totally avoid saturated fats to maintain low cholesterol.

Most vegetable oil is unsaturated fat but both saturated and unsatur-ated fats are the storage media of calories. One should minimize the consumption of unsaturated fat in their diet.

A healthy diet is made up of pure vegetarian foods (vegan) without any oil or fried food. A person will not have any cholesterol problem with this diet.

In summary, the additional cholesterol, consumed through animal and dairy products or generated by our liver due to the consumption of saturated fat, is accumulated in our blood and deposited in our arteries, which causes heart attack.

Vitamin B-12

Vitamin B-12 is needed for healthy blood and nerves. However, the body needs only 2 micro grams of B-12 per day. Vitamin B-12 is not produced by plants or by animals but by the bacteria in the digestive system of animals and humans.

Even though humans produce B-12 in their digestive systems, the human body cannot absorb its own B-12. However, cows can easily absorb the vitamin B-12 produced by the bacteria in their digestive system. Hence, there exists lots of vitamin B-12 in meat and dairy products.

If you are a vegan (absolutely no animal products), you may not be able to get enough vitamin B-12. If you get B-12 from animal products, you will also get a whopping dose of cholesterol and fat, which displaces the complex carbohydrates and fiber that the body needs and which are provided by a vegetarian diet.

Hence, vegetarians should get B-12 from other than animal products; such as fortified cereal, other fortified products, multiple vitamins, one a day vitamins, and other products from health stores which contain B-12.

Milk and Prostate Cancer

In 1997, the World Cancer Research Fund and the American Institute for Cancer Research concluded that dairy products should be considered a possible contributor to prostate cancer. Also, another research study in April 2000 pointed to a link between dairy and prostate cancer: Harvard's Physicians' Health Study followed 20,885 men for 11 years, and found that just two and a half dairy servings each day boosted prostate cancer risk by 34 percent, compared to having less than a half a serving daily.

Also dairy (milk, cheese, ice-cream), eggs, meat, and other animal products are linked to other types of cancers. They contain plenty of fat to harbor cancer-causing chemicals and promote cancer causing hormones in our body. They are low in cancer-fighting antioxidants and have no fiber. Fiber is found only in plant base food and it would normally sweep carcinogens from our digestive tract.

A cancer-prevention diet includes plenty of:

- Vegetables: sweet potatoes, carrots, broccoli, spinach, asparagus
- Fruits: strawberries, kiwi, melon, bananas, apples
- Whole grains: breads, cereal, oatmeal, pasta, rice
- Legumes: beans, peas, lentils

Whole grains, beans and other legumes, vegetables, and fruits are cancer fighters. Plant foods are low in fat, high in fiber, and loaded with protective cancer-fighting nutrients. **The most healthful diets eliminate meat, dairy products, eggs, and oil (fried foods).**

My Health Data

I was 55 years old when I became vegan. I had some concern that my health would suffer if I stopped using dairy products. The following is the summary of my health data before and after I became vegan:

	Before becoming Vegan – 1995	After becoming Vegan - 1997
Cholesterol	205	160
HDL	34	42
Trigliceride	350	175

Since becoming a vegan, I feel more energetic. I do not have a calcium deficiency. However, one should monitor his/her own body chemistry after becoming vegan. My doctor is very pleased with my results and has not put me on any vitamins or calcium substitutes. My 1998 health results were equally good.

Jain Religious View

Nonviolence is the highest principle of the Jain religion. However, for our survival, the religion permits certain violence by lay people. Jain scriptures clearly indicate that:

- For our survival, the survival of our ascetics, and the survival of our scriptures, temples, libraries, and upasrayas; limited violence to one-sensed (Ekendriya) souls such as vegetables, water, fire, earth, and air are allowed only by Jain lay people (sravaks and sravikas).

- Under no circumstances violence is allowed to living beings with from two to five senses (Tras) such as animals, birds, insects, and humans, even by lay people.

- Ascetics should be totally nonviolent to all souls including the souls of vegetables, water, fire, air, and earth.

A cow is a five-sensed (Panchendriya) animal that also possesses a mind. Cruelty to five-sensed animals is considered the highest sin in Jain scriptures.

In today's high tech environment, cows are killed instantly in the production of meat. However, during milk production cows are tortured badly during the prime of their lives, and their babies (all but one female calf) are tortured for sometime and then slaughtered. Ultimately, they are slaughtered within 5 years - well before the end of their natural life-span of 15 years. Dairy cows and their babies have no chance to escape from this cruelty and death.

In conclusion cruelty to cows, in the production of milk by dairy industry or milk supplied to dairy industry like Inida, is same or worse than in meat production. By consuming dairy products we are supporting and promoting such cruelty.

Usage of Dairy Products in the Jain Temples:

Both Swetambar and Digambar sects use milk and its products in temple rituals. This is an ancient tradition. In the past (before the birth of high tech dairy farms in India, where the cows are tortured and ultimately slaughtered), the cows were treated like a part of the family and, after feeding the baby calf, leftover milk was consumed by humans. This may be the reason why milk and its products are not considered violent in the Jain scriptures.

We should reevaluate the usage of milk and its product (ghee for arti, milk and sweets for puja, etc.) in the temple rituals under the new technological environment. **The tradition should not be followed blindly. The highest Jain principle of nonviolence should not be compromised under any circumstances.**

With regards to Swetambar tradition, I can definitely say that no scriptures support the usage of milk in the tample rituals.

With rgards to Digambar tradition, Mr. Atul Khara, the past president of Jain Centre of Dallas, Texas, indicates that most of the Digmabars do not use milk in the rituals. Also, no scriptures support the use of milk and its products in rituals, Some Digambars in South India use the milk in their rituals, which is a direct influence of Hindu rituals.

When we consume dairy products for our personal use we are personally responsible for our actions and the resulting karma or sins. When dairy products are used in the temples, the entire community commits the highest sin.

Milk and other products represent certain religious symbols in the Jain rituals but these must be of a nonviolent source. The intention of our rituals is to reduce our ego, greed, anger, lust, and attachments. Milk and other dairy products derived from a violence cannot help us to grow spiritually.

In our rituals, we should substitute regular milk with simple water or Soya milk, ghee (used in deevo) for vegetable oil, sweets for various types of dry nuts, and serve only vegan meals during any religious function. Our youths will appreciate such changes in our rituals.

Note: This article was first published on the Internet (Jain-list) in August 1997. Since then, we have received much feedback from readers across the world. We have published some of these responses in an article called **What Our Readers Say** ... at the end of this book. We strongly recommend that you read it.

New York Times - article
By - J.Peder Zane
May 12, 1996

Dairy Cows - Life, Usage, and Sufferings

(New York Times)

Title: *It Ain't Just for Meat; It's for Lotion*

Summary

To the lay person they are *cows* (and that is how they are referred to in the accompanying article) but to the beef industry they are steers, or castrated males, and heifers, or young females (only females that have given birth are referred to as cows).

The average animal (dead cow) at slaughter weighs 1,150 pounds. It weighs 714 pounds once the head, hooves, hide, and intestines are removed. The remaining carcass yields about 568 pounds of beef and 49 pounds of organs and gland, some of which like the liver - make their way to the dinner table. The rest (97 pounds) is mostly fat and bone, and is used to make everything from floor wax to pet food.

According to the Agriculture Department (USA), ranchers were getting about $632 per head (dead cattle) last week, while meat packers, who butcher the animals, were getting about $644 for the meat and $101 for the byproducts.

Some of the most valuable body parts, along with their common uses and recent wholesale prices appear at the end of this article.

Article

Introduction

Chopping sheep brains... That's what made the British cows mad, and could have killed the English men who ate them, scientists believe.

While American farmers and ranchers assure the public that no sheep passes their Elsies' lips, some folks might be surprised at what American livestock, swine and poultry are fatted upon. Besides corn, soy or other grains, their diets often include heaping helpings of **dried blood, pulverized feathers, crushed bone, leftover french fry grease from fast-food joints** and meat meal - which may include mashed pancreas, kidney, heart, and those parts that even packers, wouldn't dare shove into luncheon meats or head cheese.

Cannibalism down on the farm? You betcha...... baby chick is growing big and strong on what's left of mom after she's been shipped off as atomic wings, drumsticks and boned breasts.

"We use everything but the squeal, the cluck and the moo," says Dr. Raymond L. Burns, coordinator of the alternative uses program for the Kansas Department of Agriculture in Topeka.

Welcome to the world of offal, rendering and carcasses, an industry that gives a new meaning to the phrase *"You are what you eat."*

It asks: Once you have carved away the T-bone steaks and London broils, the pork chops and sides of Canadian bacon, the leg and the rack of lamb, what to do with the rest? With the **hearts, kidneys pituitary glands, horns, hoofs, toenails, skulls and intestines? How about the "paunch material" - undigested stomach contents?**

Answer: More than you can imagine. The abattoir's detritus is used in a dizzying array of products, including life-saving medicines, life-enhancing beauty aids, soaps, candy, clothing, upholstery, shoes and sporting goods. Not to mention crayons, floor waxes, antifreeze, matches, cellophane, linoleum, cement, photographic paper and weed killers.

While the renewed outbreak of mad cow disease in Britain led to no small panic as humanity imagined a world without Big Macs or Quarter Pounders, the fact is, the doomsday scenario is much worse. *"Take away cows or pigs and you change life as we know it,"* says Dr. Jerry Breiter, vice president of allied products for the American Meat Institute, a trade association.

Although mad cow disease is not a threat in the United States, there are other concerns. Persistent problems are E. coli bacteria - which killed three children in 1993 because they ate undercooked hamburgers at Jack-In-The-Box restaurants - and salmonella contamination which afflicts many thousands of Americans a year. While the meat industry downplays the threat, it has taken steps to clean up its act. Most large meat plants now spray steam on carcasses to kill bacteria. They routinely check meat for microbes and have established hazard checkpoints. In addition, consumers can safeguard themselves by cooking all meat thoroughly.

Still, there are ever-present ethical questions, even for those who do not think meat is murder. *The industry's cold-eyed view of animals as products to be optimally exploited is no doubt disquieting to many people.* It's worth keeping in mind, however, that no animals are slaughtered just to make floor wax or lipstick - 80 to 90 percent of a cow or pig's value is in the meat which people eat. And, as cattle prices have slid to their lowest levels in a decade, prompting president Clinton to try to shore up beef prices last week, meat packers are all the more concerned with squeezing out every penny.

"Selling the byproducts means the difference between profit and loss for the industry, and affordable and unaffordable meat for the consumer," says Dr. Breiter. Dr. Bums adds: *"If we didn't develop markets for the byproducts, we would have to dispose of them, which would create a different set of problems."*

Visiting a modern meat-packing operation can inspire us as well as a new appreciation for vegetarianism - just as more people would probably cook at home if they could peep into the kitchen of their favorite bistro.

American Slaughterhouse Statistics

On an average day in America, the following animals/birds are killed:

Cattle	130,000
Calves	7,000
Hogs	360,000
Chickens	24,000,000

Slaughterhouse Process

Modern slaughterhouses are part assembly line, part chop shop. *An efficient plant processes 250 cows an hour, 16 hours a day,* breaking them into dozens of parts as the carcass flow down the line on steel hooks.

First, the cows are led up a ramp. Their heads are placed in a holder and they are zapped unconscious. A worker, called the "sticker," plunges a sharp blade into the animal's jugular vein. As the cow dies, the spurting blood is collected in a trough; later it is baked to a dark red powder that is protein-rich animal feed.

Next, the hooves are removed and the hide is stripped for sale as leather and suede (if the cow is pregnant, the unborn calf's hide is stripped to make the top grade of leather, called slunk). Then the head is sliced off, the chest split open and the internal organs removed.

The organs - called offal - are sent to the offal room and placed on something akin to a conveyor belt, where workers in splattered smocks segregate the parts: one group collects stomach linings, another lungs. Other workers remove hearts, pancreases or thyroids. Most of the bones and hooves are rendered - that is, baked **to make bone meal, fertilizer and high-protein animal feed;** the rest are sold, primarily to manufacturers of **collagen, gelatin and pet toys.**

Slaughterhouse Products

A parallel process operates in the "fabrication area" where workers carve away the edible meats - the round, the top round, the loin, strip steaks, rib, chuck. Like car parts, each piece of the animal has its own price and market. Cow lips (which sell for 58 cents a pound) for the most part are shipped to Mexico, where they are shredded, spiced, grilled and used for taco filling.

Many cow hearts (27 cents a pound), are exported to Russia to make sausage. Much of the meat from the cow's cheek (55 cents a pound), is sold to American meat processors for sausage and baloney. Of course, many of these "variety meats" are sold to pet-food companies, which prefer to buy the separated parts.

"Just as a chef uses precise proportions to make a fine meal, the pet-food people follow recipes calling for different quantities of hearts, livers and so forth to get the right taste and nutritional content," says Mark Klein, a spokesman for Cargill, the Minneapolis-based meat packing company.

Until the rise of biotechnology - which allows drug companies to *"ferment"* medications in the laboratory using recombinant DNA - many pharmaceuticals were extracted from animals. Nevertheless, fetal blood from cows (roughly $40 to $50 a quart) remains an important tool **for the development of drugs and medical research.**

Other medications - and markets - are made by extracting hormones and other compounds from the cow's glands. The pituitary glands ($19.50 a pound) are collected **to make medicines that control blood pressure and heart rate. Twenty different steroids are made from fluids pulled from the adrenal glands ($2.85 a pound).** The lungs (6 cents a pound) go into Heparin, an anti-coagulant. And **the pancreas (63 cents a pound) is still a source of insulin for** diabetics allergic to the synthetic kind; it takes about 26 cows to maintain one diabetic for a year.

The highest price is fetched by the most dubious product – cattle gallstones, which are sold for $600 an ounce to merchants in the Far East who peddle them as an aphrodisiac.

It is no small paradox that much of the excess gristle and fat is sold to companies that promise to make people beautiful. Lipstick, makeup bases, eyeliners, eyebrow pencils, hair rinses and bubble baths wouldn't be the same without fat-derived tongue twisters like butyl stearate, glycol stearate and PEG150 distearate.

Collagen, a protein extracted from the hides, hooves and bones, is the key ingredient in age-defying moisturizers and lotions; dermatologists inject it into people's faces to fill out crows feet and laugh lines. It is also used to make breast implants and as a medium in which cells can be grown.

Soaps may trumpet their use of cocoa butter and exotic plant extracts, but most are still made from animal fats. Indeed, the word soap is said to derive from Mount Sapo, a prime spot for animal sacrifice in ancient Rome. The locals who washed their tunics in the nearby valley streams noticed that the runoff of animal fat and ashes made their whites whiter and their colors brighter....

During the last 30 years, fewer Americans have had the hankering to dine on cow brains, pig's feet and bull testicles. But our appetite for hooves - which are used to make gelatin, is insatiable. An odorless, tasteless protein, gelatin is used in hundreds of products including Gummy Bears, ice cream, hard candies and, of course, Jell-O. It is also the secret behind many "fat free" products. *"Gelatin gives the creamy mouth feel people want without the calories,"* says John Barrows, manager of marketing communications for Nabisco Inc.

A back-to-nature movement among **pet lovers has created another expanding** market for animal by products. Squeaky plastic toys are giving way to knuckle joints and beef tendons, ox tails and toenails, chew hooves and 10-pound mammoth bones taken from cows' thighs.

Which leaves one question. What do they do with the undigested paunch material? Until now, not much. But Dr. Bums of the Kansas Department of Agriculture says, there's an exciting development just around the corner. *"I can't spill the beans just yet,"* he says. *"But pretty soon we'll announce a new process for converting it back into animal feed."*

A Cow's Body Parts-Common Usage and Selling Price

Cows Body Part	Price in $/lb	Common Usage
Bones	0.42	Gelatin, Collagen Bonemeals
Tallow (fat)	0.19	Cosmetics Candles, Soap, Floor wax
Ovaries	7.50	Medication to regulate menstrucation
Hide	0.75	Footwear, Upholstery and Cloths
Hooves	0.42	Gelatin and Collagen
Horn	0.42	Gelatin and Collagen
Kidney	0.17	Humain Consumption and Pet food
Thyroid	2.00	Medicines
Trachea	0.20	Pet food
Lungs	0.06	Heparin, an anti-coagulant
Pancreas	0.63	Insulin and Pet food
Adrenal gland	2.85	Sources of 20 steroids
Spleen	0.12	Human consumption
Femur	0.42	Bones for fogs
Intestines	0.21	Human consumption
Stomach lining	0.41	Human consumption
Heart	0.27	Sausage
Lips	0.58	Taco filling
Cheek	0.55	Sausage and Baloney
Dried blood	4.40	High protein animal feed, Drug research
Liver	0.43	Human corsumption, Vitamin B-12 Heparin
Tail	1.39	Human consumption
Pituitary gland	19.50	Medicine blood prssure/heartrate
Gallstones	600.00/oz	Jewellary and Aphrocisiace

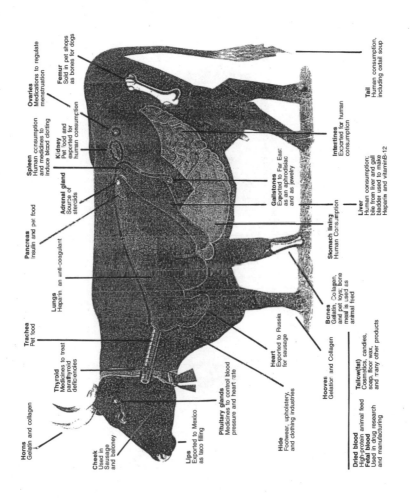

Ovaries
Medications to regulate menstruation

Femur
Sold in pet shops as bones for dogs

Tail
Human consumption, including oxtail soup

Spleen
Human consumption and medicines to induce blood clotting

Kidney
Pet food and exported for human consumption

Intestines
Exported for human consumption

Adrenal gland
Source of steroids

Gallstones
Exported to Far East as an aphrodisiac and as jewelry

Pancreas
Insulin and pet food

Liver
Human consumption; bile from liver and gall bladder used to make Heparin and vitaminB-12

Lungs
Heparin an anti-coagulant

Stomach lining
Human Consumption

Trachea
Pet food

Bones
Gelatin, Collagen, and pet toys; bone meal is used as animal feed

Thyroid
Medicines to treat parathyroid deficiencies

Heart
Exported to Russia for sausage

Horns
Gelatin and collagen

Hooves
Gelatin and Collagen

Tallow(fat)
Cosmetics, candies, soap, floor wax, and many other products

Pituitary glands
Medicines to control blood pressure and heart rate

Cheek
Used in Sausage and baloney

Hide
Footwear, upholstery, and clothing industries

Lips
Exported to Mexico as taco filling

Dried blood
High-protein animal feed

Fetal blood
Used in drug research and manufacturing

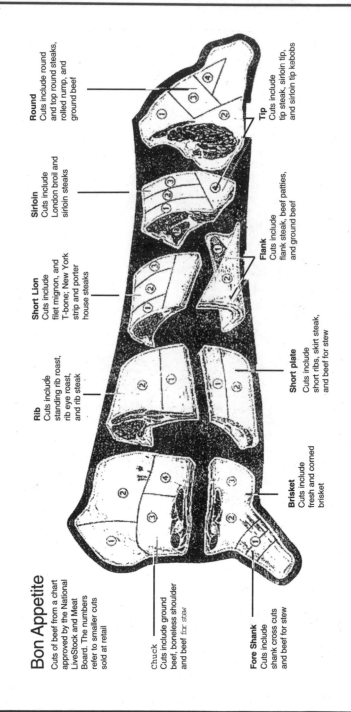

Round
Cuts include round and top round steaks, rolled rump, and ground beef

Tip
Cuts include tip steak, sirloin tip, and sirloin tip kebobs

Sirloin
Cuts include London broil and sirloin steaks

Flank
Cuts include flank steak, beef patties, and ground beef

Short Loin
Cuts include filet mignon, and T-bone; New York strip and porter house steaks

Rib
Cuts include standing rib roast, rib eye roast, and rib steak

Short plate
Cuts include short ribs, skirt steak, and beef for stew

Brisket
Cuts include fresh and corned brisket

Bon Appetite
Cuts of beef from a chart approved by the National LiveStock and Meat Board. The numbers refer to smaller cuts sold at retail

Chuck
Cuts include ground beef, boneless shoulder and beef for stew

Fore Shank
Cuts include shank cross cuts and beef for stew

Pravin K. Shah
Jain Study Center of North Carolina (Raleigh)

Recycling of Slaughterhouse Waste

(Rendering Plants)

By reading this article you will realize that dairy cows are no longer vegetarians. The dairy industry feeds them recycled meat mixed with their regular grain feed. The recycled meat is derived by recycling slaughterhouse waste, dead animals (such as millions of euthanized cats and dogs from veterinarians and animal shelters) and supermarket and restaurant waste.

Rendering Plants

Rendering plants perform one of the most valuable functions on earth. They recycle dead animals, slaughterhouse waste, supermarket and restaurant rejects into various products known as recycled meat, bone meal, and animal fat. These products are used as a source of protein and other nutrients in the diets of dairy animals (cows etc.), poultry, swine, pet foods, cattle feed, and sheep feed. Animal fat is also used in animal feeds as an energy source.

One estimate states that some 40 billion pounds a year of slaughterhouse waste like blood, bone, and viscera, as well as the remains of millions of euthanized cats and dogs passed along by veterinarians and animal shelters, are rendered annually into livestock feed. Because of this, they turn dairy cows, other cattle and hogs, which are natural herbivores (vegetarians), into unwitting carnivores.

Without rendering plants, our cities would run the risk of becoming filled with diseased and rotting carcasses. Fatal viruses and bacteria would spread uncontrolled through the population.

"If you burned all the carcasses, you'd get a terrible air pollution problem," or *"If you put it all into landfills, you'd have a colossal public health problem, not to mention stench. Dead animals are an ideal medium for bacterial growth,"* said Dr. William Heuston, associate dean of the Virginia-Maryland College of Veterinary Medicine at College Park, MD USA.

This is a multibillion-dollar industry. These facilities operate 24 hours a day just about everywhere in America, Europe and other parts of the world. They have been in operation for years. Yet so few of us have ever heard of them.

Raw Material

The dead animals and slaughterhouse waste which rendering plants recycle includes:

- Slaughterhouse waste such as heads, hooves, blood, stomachs, intestines, spinal cords, tails, feathers, and bones from cattle, sheep, pigs and horses,

- Thousands of euthanized cats and dogs from veterinarians and animal shelters

- Dead animals such as skunks, rats, and raccoons

- Carcasses of pets, livestock, poultry waste

- Supermarket and Restaurant rejected food items

Renderers in the United States pick up **100 million pounds** of waste material every day in USA. Half of every butchered cow and a third of every pig is not consumed by humans. An estimated six to seven million dogs and cats are killed in animal shelters each year, said Jeff Frace, a spokesman for the American Society for the Prevention of Cruelty to Animals in New York City. Along with the above material, the Rendering plants unavoidably process toxic wastes as indicated below.

Toxic Waste

The following menu of unwanted ingredients often accompanies dead animals and other raw material:

- Pesticides via poisoned livestock

- Euthanasia drugs that was given to pets

- Some dead animals have flea collars containing organophosphate insecticides

- Fish oil laced with bootleg DDT

- Insecticide Dursban in the form of cattle insecticide patches.

- Other chemicals leaked from antibiotics in livestock,

- Heavy metals from pet ID tag, surgical pins and needles.

- Plastic from the styrofoam trays of packaged, unsold supermarket meats, chicken and fish; cattle ID tags; plastic insecticide patches; green plastic bags containing dead pets from veterinarians.

Skyrocketing labor costs are one of the economic factors forcing the corporate flesh-peddlers to cheat. It is far too costly for plant personnel to cut off flea collars or unwrap spoiled T-bone steaks. Every week, millions of packages of plastic-wrapped meat go through the rendering process and become one of the unwanted ingredients in animal feed.

Recycled Process

The rendering plant floor is piled high with 'raw product' all waiting to be processed. In the 90-degree heat, the piles of dead animals seem to have a life of their own as millions of maggots swarm over the carcasses.

First the raw material is cut into small pieces and then transported to another auger for fine shredding. It is then cooked at 280 degrees for one hour. This continuous batch cooking process which melts the meat away from bones goes on non-stop for 24 hours a day, seven days a week

During the cooking process of the 'hot soup', yellow grease or tallow (animal fat) rises to the top and is skimmed off. The cooked meat and bone are sent to a hammermill press which squeezes out the remaining moisture and pulverizes the product into a gritty powder. Shaker screens remove excess hair and large bone chips. Now the following three products are produced:

- Recycled meat
- Yellow grease (animal fat or tallow)
- Bone meal

Since these foods are exclusively used to feed animals, most American state agencies just spot check and test for truth in labeling such as; does the percentage of protein, phosphorous and calcium match the rendering plant's claims?; do the percentages meet state requirements? Testing for pesticides and other toxins in animal feeds is incomplete or not done.

Recycled Products and Usage

Every day, hundreds of rendering plants across the United States truck millions of tons of this 'food enhancer' to the dairy industry, poultry ranches, cattle feed-lots, hog farms, fish-feed plants, and pet-food manufacturers. This food enhancer is mixed with other ingredients to feed the billions of animals.

Rendering plants have different specialties. Some product-label names are: meat meal, meat by-products, poultry meal, poultry by-products, fishmeal, fish oil, yellow grease, tallow, beef fat and chicken fat.

A 1991 USDA report states that approximately 7.9 billion pounds of meat, bone meal, blood meal, and feather meal was produced by rendering plants in 1983. Of that amount:

- 12 percent in dairy and beef cattle feed (cows)
- 34 percent was used in pet food
- 34 percent in poultry feed
- 20 percent in pig food

Scientific American cites a dramatic rise in the use of animal protein in commercial dairy feed since 1987.

At least 250 rendering plants operate in the United States and modern rendering plants are large and centralized. The industry's revenues amount to $2.4 billion a year, said Bruce Blanton, executive director of the National Renderers Association in Alexandria, Virginia.

Scientists believe the so-called mad cow disease results when cattle eat feed made from the brains or spinal cords of sheep suffering from scrapie. They believe the people who died were infected when they ate beef, or dairy or other products from these cows, a theory that remains controversial, though evidence is accumulating.

The Story of North Carolina - USA

An article entitled "Greene County Animal Mortality Collection Ramp", states that: *"With North Carolina ranking in the top seven states in the U.S. in the production of turkeys, hogs, broilers and layers, it has been recently estimated that over 85,000 tons of farm poultry and swine mortality must be disposed of annually."*

To meet this disposal need, in 1989 the Green County Livestock Producers Association began using an animal carcass collection site. Livestock producers bring the dead animal and bird carcasses to the ramp and drop them into a water-tight truck with separate compartments for poultry and other livestock parked behind the retaining wall.

A local farmer, contracted by the Livestock Association, hauls the animal and bird mortality to the rendering plant each day and maintains the collection site. The rendering plant pays the Livestock Association each week based on the current prices of meat, bone, feather meal, and fat.

During the first 16 weeks of operation in 1989, over 1 million pounds, or a weekly average of 65,000 pounds of dead animals and birds (mortality), were collected and sent to the rendering plant.

The end result of this very successful project is that Greene County livestock and poultry producers have a convenient, safe, and economical alternative to dispose of animal and bird mortality.

The Times of India
Tuesday 11 April 2000
By Pritish Nandy
(Edited and formatted for American readers)

Milk – its impact on Health, Cruelty, and Pollution

Ayurveda actually lists milk as one of the *'five white poisons'*. She has stirred a hornet's nest with her campaign against milk. Even hardcore veggies have attacked Menaka Gandhi and religious leaders have openly come out to contradict her. **Curiously, on her side now is global research and modern science, of which she has been a long-term critic.** They are the ones who are defending her now.

You have come out very strongly against milk. Why are you so hostile to it?

There are three reasons.

- People's health is compromised by milk
- Cruelty to cows and
- Pollutants in milk

Health Issues

Would you like to explain why you think milk is unhealthy?

There is this belief that milk is a complete food and an important source of protein, iron and calcium. Milk has no iron, and also blocks its absorption. The ability of the body to absorb calcium from milk is barely 32%. Whereas the body can absorb 65% calcium from cabbage and 69% from cauliflower.

Milk has less protein than most vegetables. Even if we assume it contains more protein, it would be useless for human beings. Because human beings require only 4 to 5 percent of their daily calorie intake in proteins and the daily consumption of Indian bread (Chapattis) and potatoes would give more protein than the requirements.

So milk is not the best food in the world as it has been touted for generations?

Milk is very difficult to digest, particularly for Asians and Africans.

Why do I not eat plastic? It's because I have no enzyme to digest it. We do not have lactose in our body and so we cannot digest lactose. If we cannot digest milk, how do we get any of its ingredients?

Apart from this, milk has something called the IGF-1. All cancer studies show that when IGF-1 rises in the body one gets cancer. All the IGF-1 in milk stays in the body, making one prone to cancer. It is also a very strong cause of asthma. In fact, doctors recommend that asthma patients avoid milk and milk products.

The problem with doctors in India is that they are not taught nutrition in medical colleges. So, they have a limited knowledge of food. Their knowledge of nutrition comes from the same source as yours and mine: Grandmothers and teachers. Add to this the confusion caused by our local religious leaders, particularly the ones who espouse vegetarianism.

What is specifically wrong in milk? What is specifically harmful?

The calcium contained in milk actually becomes a health hazard as undigested portions of it are deposited in the urinary system and become kidney stones. Another condition that milk aggravates rather than alleviates is osteoporosis or bone loss. **Studies have shown that it is excess protein rather than lack of calcium that causes osteoporosis.** So the more milk you drink, the more you are prone to osteoporosis. Countries like Sweden that have the highest milk consumption also have the highest incidence of osteoporosis.

Another misconception is that milk helps ulcers. Ulcers are caused by the corrosion of the stomach lining. When you drink milk it gives you immediate pain relief. But that is only temporary. Milk actually causes acidity and further destroys the stomach lining.

Also, ulcer patients who are treated with dairy products are found to be 2 to 6 times more prone to heart attacks. This seems only logical because milk is designed to be the food on which a calf increases its body weight 4 times over in one month! It is so naturally high in fat that it leads to obesity, the cause of all modern disease. Ayurveda actually lists milk as one of the five white poisons.

Indians have been drinking milk for centuries. Why is it that all of them did not fall sick?

It depends on what you call illness. Most people disregard arthritis, osteoporosis, asthma, headaches, and indigestion as normal for the body and cancer as an act of God.

By looking at milk as evil, are we not turning our back on our tradition and culture?

For thousands of years people thought the sun went around the earth. Copernicus was the first person who said it did not. There was a huge backlash against him. In the past, in India there existed the tradition of sati (cremating a widow with her husband's dead body) and thugee and opium eating. Should they be legal now?

I have written a book on Hindu names for which I had to read every single Hindu scripture (shastra). Nowhere is there any milk drinking mentioned. There is ghee (liquid butter) mentioned and that too for havans (fire used in Hindu ritual). Unfortunately, our memories are short and the things we are most adamant about are those we know the least about. **Dr. Spock, the guru of child nutrition, now apologizes for having advocated milk and says that children must be kept away from it.**

Cruelty to Cows

Dr Kurien has described the dairy industry as the gentle industry. You claim it is just the opposite?

The dairy industry is not gentle. The fact that supplies cater to demand makes the cow the ultimate victim. It may have been gentle when each household had its own cow and treated it as a member of the family. This is no longer true.

How is milk produced now in India?

The cow is forced into yearly pregnancies. After giving birth, she is milked for 10 months but will be artificially inseminated during her third month so that she is milked even when she is pregnant. The demand for the production of milk is more than her body can give and she starts breaking down body tissue to produce milk. The result is an illness called ketosis.

Most of the day the cow is tied up in a narrow stall, usually wallowing in her own excrement. She gets mastitis because the hands that milk her are rough and usually unclean. She gets rumen acidosis from bad food and lameness. She is kept alive with antibiotics and hormones. Each year, 20 per cent of these dairy cows are sent illegally by truck and train to slaughterhouses. Or they are starved to death by letting them loose in the cities. It is no secret that the slaughterhouse in Goa was constructed by Amul Dairy. No cow lives out her normal life cycle. She is milked, made sick and then killed. Even worse is what happens to her calf. The male calves are tied up and starved to death or sent to the slaughter houses. It is not by chance that a calf is no longer called bachda in India. It is called katra, which means one who is to be killed. Even Dr Kurien admits that in Mumbai every year 80,000 calves are forcibly put to death.

But milkmen (doodhwalas) love their cows. They live off them.

Have you seen how cows are milked? In the villages they practice phukan, a method of milking a cow. A stick is poked into the cow's uterus and wiggled, causing her intense pain. Villagers believe this leads to more milk.

In the cities they are given two injections of oxytocin every day to make the milk come faster. This gives her labor pains twice a day. Her uterus develops sores and makes her sterile prematurely. Oxytocin is banned for use on animals but it is sold in every cigarette shop around a dairy. Every illiterate milkman knows the word. In human beings, oxytocin causes hormonal imbalances, weak eyesight, miscarriages, and cancer.

Recently, the government of Gujarat started raiding dairies for oxytocin. In one day, they found 350,000 ampoules in just one city Ahmedabad!

Pollutants in Milk

You mentioned pollution in milk. What does that mean?

The ICMR did research on milk for 7 years and took thousands of samples from across India. What did they find?

arge amounts of DDT, poisonous pesticides called HCH. Under the food adulteration act only 0.01 mg/kg is allowed of HCH. They found 5.7 mg as an average! They found arsenic, cadmium and lead. This causes kidney damage, heart disease, brain damage and cancer.

Their findings were based on 50,000 samples and the report was released at a press conference. What did Dr Kurien and the Operation Flood people have to say? More samples should have been taken!

Other things put in your milk is sewage water, vegetable oil, and liquid soap. In some cases earthworms are put in because they excrete slime which increases the density of the milk!

You have said that drinking milk is drinking the cow's blood ?

Milk and blood come from the same source; the body cells of the cow. Every time you drink a glass of milk, remember it comes from a sad, suffering mother whose own child was killed before her eyes and who herself will be killed when she dries up.

Won't the stoppage of milk lead to thousands being unemployed?

A large number of people are dependent on smuggling, thievery, begging, drug pushing, gun running and terrorism. Do we buy their products to help them?

What is the substitute for milk?

What is the substitute for a placebo? Anything else such as Soya bean milk, all green vegetables, and lentils (dal). My son has never drunk milk in his life. He is 6 feet and has never been sick a single day!

TIME Asia News Article
By MASEEH RAHMAN, New Delhi - India
MAY 29, 2000 VOL. 156 NO. 21

Is Nothing Sacred?
Cruelty towards India's Holy Animals

Headline News

International animal-rights activists expose the barbaric transport and slaughter of the country's most revered animals and accuse India of showing uncharacteristic cruelty toward its holy animals.

Article

Mahatma Gandhi believed that a nation could be judged by the way it treats its animals. If that yardstick were applied to his own country today, India would be in the doghouse. Hindus venerate many of God's creatures, and the cow is considered especially sacred. But the international animal-rights group, People for the Ethical Treatment of Animals (PETA), has exposed horrendous cruelty to India's cows as they are illegally transported illegally to slaughterhouses. Many arrive dead or badly injured after long and torturous journeys in trains and trucks or on foot. *"It is Dante's Inferno for cows and bullocks,"* says PETA president Ingrid Newkirk.

India's livestock population, estimated at more than 500 million, is the world's largest. More than half is cows, buffaloes, and bulls. Once they become unproductive, many of the animals are sold by their owners, mostly subsistence farmers, and marched off to slaughter houses.

Cow slaughter is permitted in just two provinces, the communist-ruled states of **West Bengal** in the east and **Kerala** in the south. Although it is illegal to transport the animals for slaughter across state borders, traders bribe officials to look the other way as they pack the cows into rail cars or trucks headed for West Bengal or Kerala. The animals frequently gore one another or break their pelvises when forced to jump from the trucks. Some suffocate inside boxcars. Thousands of others are surreptitiously herded overland— often without food or water. If they collapse from exhaustion, herders break their tails or throw chili pepper and tobacco in their eyes to make them walk again.

The campaign against the practice is attracting support from a number of animal-activist celebrities. Paul McCartney, Brigitte Bardot, Steven Seagal and Nina Hagen took part in an international day of protest the second week of May 2000, in their home countries. **"My heart breaks for the misery endured by the entire population of mother cows and their calves ... who have become throw-away in today's India," McCartney declared.**

The $1.6 billion Indian leather export industry is feeling the pinch. Companies such as Gap and its subsidiaries Banana Republic and Old Navy have banned the use of Indian leather in their garments. The British Shoe Company, Clark's, announced last week that it would review the purchase of products made from Indian leather. PETA's list also includes Florsheim, Nordstrom, Casual Corner and other retail chains. *"It's a wake-up call to India's leather industry,"* says PETA's Indian campaign coordinator Jason Baker. *"If it doesn't do something soon to stop the cruelty against cows, there will be no leather industry left."*

India's leather barons are worried that the protests will cripple exports to the West. Nearly 4,000 tanneries and leather-goods factories depend on the export trade. The industry employs around 1.7 million people; nearly a third of whom are women. *"The campaign is going to affect us, no doubt about it,"* says Mohammed Hashim, chairman of the Council for Leather Exports. He feels his tribe is unfairly targeted. *"We are only scavengers,"* he says. *"We take skins sold by slaughter houses."* Moreover, he adds, 90% of the hides used are from buffalo, goats or sheep. His organization has appealed to exporters to use only leather from animals that have been killed humanely.

The government, though, shows no sign of moving against the illegal transport and slaughter. Before PETA's campaign, Indian animal-rights groups had been trying for years to stop the brutal cattle trail. It's a multimillion-dollar business, and the kickbacks to politicians and officials are thought to be huge (The bovine "death trains" are operated by the state-owned railway). Banning cow slaughter in West Bengal and Kerala probably wouldn't help, as it would surely lead to an increase in the number of illegal, back-street slaughter houses. New Delhi may simply find it easier to respond to other demands by animal lovers, like creating a national authority for protecting cows or introducing tougher penalties for cruelty to animals (under existing law, the fine is only about $1).

A simpler solution would be to lift the ban on cow slaughter throughout

India, to deter the deadly, illegal herding across state lines. *"Villagers can't afford to keep unproductive cows. They're not saints,"* says Bangalore animal-welfare worker Suparna Baksi-Ganguly. *"Slaughter has to be made more accessible —suppressing it, causes greater misery to the animals."* But such a step would provoke the ire of cow lovers, and no political party is likely to risk that. So, in a land that venerates them, cows will continue to pay a high price for their holiness.

Pramoda Chitrabhanu
Jain Meditation International Center, New York

Vegetarianism
A Compassionate Approach to Life

"Unseen they suffer, unheard they cry.

In agony they linger, in silence they die.

Is it nothing to you, all ye who pass by?"

-Anonymous

These lines express the pain and suffering of the animals that are being exploited and tortured for the need of the human greed.

It is a sad picture of the innocent, dumb and defenseless creatures that are subjected to cruel pain far from the human eyes. The thought itself makes one's heart bleed with anguish and grief. How can we as human beings sit quietly when our younger brothers and sisters are in terrible state? Is it not our duty to protect and help them? But how difficult it is to predict man for, *"Man is an actor. He acts all manners of men, and each one is a lie. Only the animal in him is real,"* says William Saroyan. Probably he is right by saying that, for the beastiality in the man has created a violent and destructive world in which we live today.

There is so much suffering going on in this world behind the curtain that it is kept a highly guarded secret. How long shall we pretend that animals have no soul and so it feels no pain. Is it not the time to wake up from our slumber and find the truth and stop being violent and act to end the cruelty that is meted on the dumb and innocent creatures? For violence begets violence and love begets love.

The first thing to end violence is to see animals as living beings and not as things that are made for human beings to use and consume. For they are lives full of emotions that feel pain and pleasure as we do. As Dr. Albert Schweitzer the Nobel Peace Prize Recipient in 1952 said in his book ***A Place for Revelation*** that *"**wherever you see life - that is you**. What is this recognition, this knowledge apprehended by the most learned and most childlike alike? It is 'Reverence for Life,' reverence for the impenetrable mystery that meets us* *in our universe, an existence different from ourselves in external appearance yet inwardly of the same character with us. Terribly similar, awesomely related. This dissimilarity, the strangeness between us and other creatures are here removed. Reverence before the infinity of life means the removal of the strangeness, the restoration of shared experiences, and of compassion and sympathy."*

In this way when we learn to see the animals as ourselves we change our perception of them and become more compassionate towards them. When such an understanding dawns on us, the first change occurs in the food pattern. One then starts to observe what one puts into the body where the soul is housed. For we know that, we are what we eat. What we eat reflects in our thinking and our thinking reflects in our action. If we want a healthy body and a healthy mind, the body should be provided with healthy and wholesome food, pure and untainted by blood and negative vibrations. One is often not aware of the fact that when one eats meat, one takes in protein as well as the chemicals that are injected into the animals to fatten them up and to control diseases and viruses. One also forgets that in flesh, the negative vibrations of pain, fear and rejection do exist, and they permeate every cell of the human body creating there the feeling of fear, pain and rejection.

How does one hope to live with good feelings of health, happiness and sound mind when negative vibrations of pain blended with chemicals are working in the body? These are the causes that lead to the fatal diseases of the mind and the body. That is the reason why we see so many people suffering from psychological and physiological diseases.

Statistically, approximately two million Americans die each year of which 68% are victims of the three major chronic diseases in which diet is major contributory factor: heart disease, cancer and stroke. The foods that have been singled out for special concern in connection with these diseases are eggs, meat, poultry, sea- food, animal fat and many more. So, feeding the body with food that involves minimum of violence, environmental damage and ecological imbalance creates harmony within and harmony without.

It is good to know the following statistics :

● It takes 273 liters of water to produce 450 grams of wheat.

● 1136.5 liters of water to produce 450 grams of rice.

● 9000 to 27,000 liters of water to produce 450 grams of meat.

● A chicken processing plant uses 454 million liters per day enough to supply the water needs of 25,000 humans.

- Livestock are responsible for consuming 80% of the world's water supply (A liter is 4 ½ cups of liquid).

Methane from cattle accelerates the global warming and the ozone layer depletion. PETA's (People for the Ethical Treatment of Animal) research shows that 26 billion animals are killed for food in the U.S. alone each year (9 billion land based, 17 billion aquatic). In this way when man lives a life involving gross violence he becomes a threat to himself and to the entire planet.

But if one becomes a vegetarian (Vegan meaning absolutely no animal products) he saves 2,400 animals in a lifetime thus becoming a blessing to oneself and a blessing to the Mother Earth. Today, people all over the world are slowly becoming aware of the animal abuse and torture and are becoming vegetarians. Some for religious purpose, some for ethical reason, some for ecological reason and some for health or environmental point of view. The awareness is gaining momentum day by day. If one can try this way of diet for few months one can find out for themselves if there is any change in their state of mind and the body.

Let us see what vegetarianism means in today's world. The term Vegetarian is derived from the Latin word vegetus meaning *"whole, lively, sound, fresh."* Thus a vegetarian is one who does not eat any meat, fish, fowl or eggs. There are those who consider themselves to be vegetarians even though they eat eggs. So the vegetarians are divided into following categories:

Lacto-ovo-vegetarians	Vegetarians diet includes milk, other dairy products, and eggs.
Lacto-vegetarians	Vegetarian diet includes milk, dairy products, but no eggs.
Vegans	Vegetarian diet does not include any animal products like milk, cheese, yogurt (curd), butter or eggs, and honey. In addition they avoid wearing leather, wool, silk and use of other animal products.
Eggitarian	A lacto - vegetarian who would not eat eggs explicity, but will eat cookies, cakes etc. that may contain eggs.

A vegetarian (Vegan - absolutely no animal products) can easily sustain on foods like grains, legumes, beans, nuts, seeds, vegetables and fruits that are good sources of protein, vitamins, minerals and other nutrients. We just saw the ethical, ecological and health point of view of vegetarianism. Now let us address the philosophical aspect of the issue.

Since time immemorial scriptural studies and research have revealed one thing that is common to all living beings and that is the desire to live and to be happy. It says that no one wants to be unhappy or in pain. But man in his pursuit of pleasure and happiness goes to the extent of using everything and everyone for his greed and satisfy his yearning by engaging in violent acts like hunting, killing, confining, or taking the life of freely roving innocent creatures. In this way, not only does he abuse the living creatures, but in turn abuses himself. For he too is a living creature and cannot remove him self from the universal law of vibrations of the living which is, what you throw out comes about.

To kill someone you have to be callous and then kill that life. When one acts in unawareness one kills the goodness in one's self and reaches a point of hating the self. If one does not have reverence for one's own self, how can one have reverence for other living beings? In this way violence perpetuates and the vicious circle of hate and violence continues.

One never stops to think that eating meat for taste involves much pain and torture to a life! A life that cannot be created in the laboratory! A very precious life with a strong will to live! A life that needs time to unfold its own destiny on earth, for a premature death breaks the cycle of natural expression of life. The philosopher Plutarch said, "But for the sake of some little mouthful of flesh, we deprive a soul of the life and time it had been born into the world to enjoy."

Very often people ask the question, *"Why then, kill vegetables if not animals?"* The Jain school of thought answers this question precisely. Basically this universe is made up two substances, i.e., *"living"* and *"non-living."* Living substance means human beings, animals, birds, insects, smaller organisms, vegetation, air, water and earth. Non-living substances are tables, chairs, buildings, trains, cars, machines, etc. Wherever there is life, there is consciousness, there is the feeling of pain, a response to stimuli.

According to Jain philosophy, all life is divided into five categories according to the number of the senses they possess, such as one-sense beings to five-sense beings having the sense of touch, taste, smell, sight and hearing. The more the number of senses the more evolved the life is. Vegetables are one-sense beings having the sense of touch and animals are five-sense beings having all the five senses. Life has to go through a laborious and strenuous process to evolve from one sense beings to five-sense beings. By slaughtering an animal one destroys completely the evolutionary progress of that life, which it has attained through suffering and pain. The vegetable kingdom has not yet reached the blood *"consciousness"* which the animals and humans have. So the degree of pain is less. Where there is blood, there are more feelings, more emotions and possibility to feel deep pain. So one agrees that for living violence is inevitable, but one has the choice to minimize violence.

Two thousand and six hundred years ago, Mahavir, the great exponent of non-violence and compassion emphasized that thoughts that govern our actions are the products of the food we eat. The food that feeds the system has a definite influence on the person physically as well emotionally, psychologically and spiritually. Healthy, whole and harmless foods give rise to healthy whole and harmless thoughts. Once the thoughts are harmless and healthy, the actions also reflect the same qualities. Weakness in character always develops in those who are in poor health, mentally or physically.

Science has discovered in recent years that character and personality are attributes of the inner workings of the body and have a great bearing upon our success in life and in our happiness. The personality reveals and expresses itself through the physical body. The expression of the face, the smile, which is the manifestation of joy, happiness and compassion, reveal the personality within. Without a healthy body, these manifestations are not possible.

Thus vegetarianism is one of the many ways of expressing our reverence for all life forms including ourselves- from the minutest micro-beings to the macro- beings, from the lowest developed consciousness to the highest developed consciousness.

Pramoda Chitrabhanu
Jain Meditation International Center, New York

Varakh (Silver Foil)

Do you know whether the varakh (silver foil) used in many Jain temples on the idols and in some religious ceremonies is vegetarian?

Do you know how the varakh on your sweets (mithai) is manufactured? As a child, I remember always asking for those sweets that had silver foil on them. Even today children as well as adults go for varakh on the sweets. Its popular appeal has a stronger hold on people's minds, increasing the demand and thereby its supply. If people knew the source and method of making it, I am sure they would never eat the silver-coated sweets again.

Let us find out the procedure from the article written by Beauty Without Cruelty (BWC), India branch. We are thankful to them for this valuable information.

If you look beyond the glitter of varakh, into the sheds where it is produced, and at the lives that are sacrificed to make this possible, you would think twice before buying that box of sweets topped with the precious silver foil!

Silver foil, or varakh, as it is generally known in India, adds glitter to Indian sweets (mithai), supari (betel nut), paan (betel-leaf), and fruits. Also it is used in Ayurvedic medicines and on deities in many Jain temples. The silver-topped sweet is even served as prasad in temples and on auspicious and religious occasions. Varakh is also used in flavored syrups as in kesar (saffron) syrup.

Several years ago, as suggested by BWC, Indian Airlines instructed their caterers to stop the use of varakh on sweets (mithai) served on board their flights. Today, many ask for sweets without varakh, having realized the cruelty involved in its preparation.

According to a feature article in Business India, an astounding 275 tons of silver are eaten annually in foil for sweets and chyavanprash! That is a whopping 2,75,000 kilograms! (At the present market rate that would cost a phenomenal Rs. 165 Crore or $ 40 million U.S. Dollars).

Just how is varakh made and what is it that makes its preparation and consumption so sinful?

Varakh is not derived from an animal source. However, a crucial material of animal origin, ox-gut, is used in its manufacture. This ox gut is obtained from the slaughterhouses.

In the by-lanes of the villages of Ahmedabad (Gujarat state, India) and other cities, amidst filthy surroundings, placed between layers of ox-gut, small thin strips of silver are hammered to produce the glittering foil.

The intestine (ox-gut), smeared with blood and mucus, is pulled out from the slaughtered animal by the butcher at the slaughterhouse and sold for the specific purpose. Note that it is not a by-product of slaughter but, like everything else, meat, hide, and bones are sold by weight. This is then taken away to be cleaned and used in the manufacture of varakh.

The gut of an average cow, measuring 540 inches in length and 3 inches in diameter, is cut open into a piece measuring 540" x 10". From this, strips of 9" x 10" are cut to give approximately 60 pieces of ox-gut, which are then piled one onto another and bound to form a book of 171 leaves.

Next, small thin strips of silver are placed between the sheets and the book slipped into a leather pouch (note this use of an animal product again). Artisans then hammer these bundles continuously for a day to produce extremely thin foils of silver 3" x 5".

The leather and ox-gut, being supple, can withstand the intense manual hammering for up to 8 hours a day till such time as the silver is beaten to the desired thickness. When ready, the foil is carefully lifted from between the leaves of ox-gut and placed between sheets of paper to be sold to the sweet makers (mithaiwallas). A booklet of 160 foils weighs approximately 10 grams and costs about Rs. 200 ($5.00).

To make a single booklet of 171 sheets, the guts of 3 cows are used. And the yield per book is generally 160 foils of silver, the rest of which may be damaged or unfit for use. Thus, one book, used an average of 300 days of the year, yields approximately 48,000 foils of silver, which means that each ox-gut yields an estimated 16,000 foils.

The leather used for the pouch to hold the book (made from ox-gut), is cowhide or calf leather, and uses about 232 sq. inches of material.

Assuming the size of an average cowhide to be 18 sq. ft or 2,600 sq. inches, the yield per hide will be approximately 10 leather pouches.

Usually, 4 foils are used per kilograms (2.2 lbs.) of sweets and the ox-gut of one cow is used to produce foil for approximately 4,000 kilograms (9,000 lbs.) of sweets. It is estimated (by surveys) that the average consumption of sweets by a middle class family of four in India is about 100 kilograms per year. Thus, an average middle class Indian family of four, consuming approximately 100 kg of sweets per year for forty years, consumes silver foil produced with the gut of 3 cows and one-tenth of a cowhide!

India is not the only country where foil is made by such methods. In Germany, small-specialized enterprises produce gold leaf, which is beaten down to 1/10,000-millimeter thickness, for decorative and technical purposes by similar methods. The Jews use the gold foil for as much the same purposes, namely for food preparations, as it is in India.

In India the 275 tons of silver that are beaten annually into varakh utilize intestines of 516,000 cows and calf leather of 17,200 animals each year.

We hope that someone; somewhere will develop an alternative process for the making of varakh without using ox-gut.

Pramoda Chitrabhanu
Jain Meditation International Center, New York

Facts about Eggs

Do you remember as a child your mother telling you not to eat cakes or pastries that had eggs because you are a vegetarian? Many times I have heard people say that eggs are vegetarian food and are healthy so we eat them. The myths about vegetarian eggs and its health-promoting qualities are misleading. The consumption of eggs by so many vegetarians is really shocking. This ignorance has spread so far that people resist believing that an egg has potential life and that an egg has an unborn chick within its shell.

Man's desire for food has made him go to extremes and lead him to eat those foods that are colored with violence and pain. Nature has its reason for eggs, not as food for man but as an important link in the reproductive system of hens. It is the craving for violent food that actually numbs the feeling and thinking capacity of the human being. He ignores going deep into the subject and shuns the truth of the matter. But how long will he remain in darkness? For facts are facts and they will never change whether he accepts them or not.

Let us look at some facts about eggs and remove the ignorance that prevails in our mind. The facts you are about to read are taken from the book, *A Hundred Facts about Eggs,* by Dr. Nemi Chand.

Eggs of all birds are structurally alike (See the McDonald Encyclopedia of Birds of the World, Page 30-31). Their internal structure is meant for reproduction of progeny and not for human consumption. By eating eggs, man has reverted to the hunting stage of his civilization. He is meddling both with nature and with the reproductive system.

The egg is totally forbidden for those who believe in non-violence. Right from the rearing of hens to the hatching of their eggs, there is violence all over. A visit to any poultry farm will support this fact. In poultry farms, hens are considered no better than egg-producing machines. They are confined to a narrow space of 15ö x 19ö in the midst of several hardships and tensions that are naturally passed on to the blood and system of those who eat their eggs and turn them into imbalanced personalities.

Chickens are housed in small, congested cages known as chicken-havens. Due to a shortage of space, they naturally become violent, offensive, obsessed and quarrelsome. They attack one another in a barbarous manner. So they are de-beaked. Due to de-beaking, they are unable even to drink water. Do we not realize the cause of our present widespread complexes, aggressiveness and suffering in the chicken-havens?

As mentioned earlier, hens are de-beaked to prevent them from fighting and wounding one another. The de-beaking is done in brown light, especially during the night when hens become almost blind. The lower beak is cut. If any mistake is made, the hen is deprived of food for the rest of her life. The hen has to starve at least for three days due to the wounded beak. Wouldn't this act of cruelty affect the egg-eater?

Hens are given five kinds of violence-generating foods: bone meal, blood-meal, excreta-food, meat-meal and fish-meal. Can we dare to call eggs vegetarian food even after learning this?

The term vegetarian egg is a first-rate misnomer. The purpose of a fertile egg is to animate life, but an infertile egg has no such purpose and as such should be considered totally inedible. Battery and factory eggs are harmful to health. It is better that we abstain ourselves from eating them.

The egg produced without any contact with the male bird (an infertile egg) is also animate because it is born out of the hen's body with its blood and cells. Therefore, its consumption is 100% non-vegetarian.

According to the famous American scientist, Mr. Philip J. Scamble, no egg is without life in it. The scientists at Michigan University in America have proven beyond a doubt that no egg - fertile or infertile - is without life (inanimate).

The hen gives infertile eggs during the absence of the male bird. But it has been observed that she gives an infertile egg before the day of contact with the male bird - and also the next day. In other words, she can give a fertile egg even without contact with a male bird. On the fifth day, again she gives a fertile egg. This means that the semen of the male bird remains lying in her body for a considerable duration. In some cases, this duration has been observed to be as long as even six months.

A fertilized egg is a pre-birth stage of a chicken; unfertilized eggs are the result of the sexual cycle of a hen and very unnatural. Both are non-vegetarian food. Victoria Moran, the author of the book *Compassion: The Ultimate Ethics* says that to eat a fertilized egg is in fact to consume a chicken before its birth (The Ethic on borderline). I was told that an unfertilized egg is the product of a bird's sexual cycle and can hardly be regarded as natural food for Man.

Whether the egg is fertile or infertile, life is essentially there; and it has all the symptoms of life, such as respiration, brain, feeding ability, etc. There are 15,000 porous-breathing holes on the shell, the cover of the egg. The egg begins to rot at a temperature of less than 8^ Celsius, 00^ Fahrenheit. When it begins this process, its rotting manifests itself through evaporation of the water content. The egg becomes infected by germs and thus becomes diseased. The progress of the rotting soon reaches the shell of the egg.

Eggs contain cholesterol in large quantities. The yellow bulk of the egg is the major source of cholesterol. Cholesterol narrows down the arteries and may eventually lead to a heart attack or to paralysis. Eating eggs may also lead to rheumatism and gout that can cause serious and painful joints in old age.

All the above facts lead to prove that eggs are not vegetarian and so let us re-think about the issue of eggs and realize that a balanced vegetarian diet contains an abundance of health-protecting nutrients and fibers without eggs.

Pramoda Chitrabhanu
Jain Meditation International Center

THE STORY OF SILK

How many people know that the silk one wears or uses involves violence and that one wears it with great pride in the places of worship? It is sad that one follows traditions blindly without questioning the origination or it's making process.

It all started around 1133 AD at the time of King Kumarpal, the King of Gujarat, a state in Western India. During his rule he was greatly influenced by a great Jain teacher Acharya Hemchandra. The King was so inspired by his teachings of Ahimsa (nonviolence) and Compassion that he declared in his entire state to stop killing for food, sport or fun.

It is said that he was further inspired by the saint to lead a religious life and perform puja (a symbolic worship to an idol in the temple) everyday to show his devotion to Lord Mahavir. The King decided to wear the best and most expensive new clothes to perform the puja. His men went and purchased the most costly, fine and soft material from China for their King. At that time, the King did not know that the material purchased for him was imported silk, made from killing silkworms, which involved sheer violence. If he knew that he would not have used silk for puja. But since then, the tradition continues. Unfortunately, even today, people wear silk clothes in religious rituals justifying that King Kumarpal used it.

It is time one wakes up to the fact and knows the true story of silk. **Beauty Without Cruelty** organization in India has done great work in this field and brought to light the cruelty involved in making silk.

Soft, smooth and shimmering, silk is perhaps the most attractive textile ever created. More than two thousand years ago, this beautiful fabric was imported from China known as "Chinanshuk" in Sanskrit language. The method and source of its production was a very highly guarded secret -maybe because it involved the killing of millions of lives.

The filament of silk is what a silkworm spins for its cocoon. The cocoon is constructed as its shell to protect itself during its cycle of growth from caterpillar to chrysalis to moth. The female moth lays about 400-600 eggs. The eggs hatch in about 10 days and the larvae (1/12 inch in length) emerge. They are fed on mulberry leaves for 20-27 days till they are fully grown (3 to 3 1/2 inches in length).

A fully-grown caterpillar emits a gummy substance from its mouth and wraps itself in layers of this filament to form a cocoon in 2 to 4 days. The caterpillar develops into a moth in about 15 days. To emerge it has to cut through the cocoon - thereby ruining the filament of the cocoon. In order to save the filaments from being broken, the chrysalis are either immersed in boiling water or passed through hot air or exposed to the scorching heat of the sun, thus killing the lives inside. The filaments of the cocoons are then reeled.

To produce 100 grams of pure silk, approximately 1,500 chrysalis have to be killed. Certain chrysalis are chosen and kept aside to allow the moths to emerge and mate. After the female moth lays eggs, she is crushed to check for diseases. If she has any disease, the eggs laid by her are destroyed. Generation after generation of inbreeding has taken away the moth's capacity to fly. After mating, the male moths are dumped into a basket and thrown out.

India produces four varieties of silks obtained from four types of moths. These are known as Mulberry, Tussar, Eri and Muga. Mulberry is also produced in other silk-producing countries: China, Japan, Russia, Italy, South Korea, etc. but Eri and Muga are produced in India only.

The other materials that look somewhat like silk are from man-made fibers known as artificial silk (art silk). Of these, rayon (viscose) is of vegetable origin; where as nylon and polyester (terrene) are petroleum products. Silk, once woven, is known by different names depending on the weave, style, design and place where it is woven. Materials like boski, pure crepe, pure chiffon, pure gaji, pure georgette, khadi silk, matka silk, organza, pure satin, etc. are 100% silk. Saris from Calcutta, Gadhwal, Madurai and Shantiniketan can be in 100% silk or 100% cotton. Irkal saris from Narayan Peth (Andhra Pradesh) can be of 100% silk or part silk and part cotton yarn.

Venkatgiri saris may be in all cotton or part silk/cotton. Chanderi, Tissue, Poona, Ventakgiri and Maheshwari Saris of Madhya Pradesh have silk yarn in warp and cotton yarn in weft. Manipuri Kota and Munga Kota have both silk and cotton yarn. Matka silk is also 100% pure silk. In this, the yarn in warp is the usual silk yarn, whereas the yarn in weft is obtained from the cocoons that are cut open by the moth to come out. Later these moths are crushed to death after they lay eggs.

Materials like crepe, chinon, chiffon, gaji, georgette, satin, etc. can be made from man-made fiber called artificial silk. Cheaper quality of Tanchhoi can contain silk yarn in warp and artificial yarn in warp and artificial yarn in weft.

Pramoda Chitrabhanu
Jain Meditation International Center, New York

THE STORY OF PEARLS

In the olden days, lustrous and beautiful natural pearls were a symbol of wealth and pride for those who owned them. When we see the ancient portraits of kings and queens with long pearl necklaces and bracelets worn around their wrists it reiterates the same fact. Today the story is different. We see that very few corners of the world are free from a hostile and violent environment. When we come to know the true story behind the pearls, it will hardly remain a sign of wealth and pride for any one. For those who care for life, the pearl is a symbol of pain and suffering.

Myths and legends hide the bitter fact that pearls come from the suffering of the oysters found deep in the ocean. Pearls are not the natural part of the living oyster but a response to an irritation caused by a foreign particle. It occurs when sand or a bit of shell or an unwelcome parasite is trapped accidentally inside the oyster's shell. It's like having a foreign particle in the human eye, causing irritation until removed.

Most of the time the oyster cannot expel the foreign particle. So to reduce the pain caused by the foreign body, it surrounds it with nacre - a silvery calcium carbonate substance that the oyster normally discharges to line it's shell.

After several years, layers of nacre form a pearl around the irritant, making the irritant less painful. This way the oyster creates a rainbow like iridescent pearl. Due to this natural process pearls were rarely found.

Driven by greed, men then invented artificial ways to obtain more pearls. One such man is Kokichi Mikimoto who experimented for years to produce pearls in oysters. In the early 1900's he found the solution and discovered the method of commercial pearl culturing in Japan.

A painful journey of the oyster begins. Mikimoto patented a way of tricking small akoya oysters into producing pearls. The process begins with divers searching for young oysters in the deep ocean. A technician then takes a round bead made from the shell of the fresh water mussel. This bead is called the nucleus that substitutes the foreign particle and is inserted into the oyster. Then a tiny piece of mantle (oyster's fleshy lip) is cut from the same oyster and inserted next to the nucleus. All this is done without anesthesia. This nucleus causes pain and irritation to the inside of the oyster for years. This pain causes the mantle to secrete the nacre that coat the nucleus until it has formed into a pearl. Such "seeded" pearls are consistently rounder and more luminous and, more importantly, they can be produced in larger quantities for human greed and passion. For years the oyster suffers the hurt and soreness until the oyster is split open alive to get the pearl. Many a times an oyster may yield nothing at all and the life is ended.

After knowing the process of the real and cultured pearls, the belief that pearls do not involve any violence turns false. Many believe that cultured pearls are man-made, simulated or fake pearls made by machines. The truth proved otherwise: they are made and produced solely by oysters and obtained by killing millions of oysters each year mercilessly.

Pramoda Chitrabhanu
Jain Meditation International Center, New York

The Myth About Milk

Since our childhoods, we have been made to believe that milk gives nourishment and is good for the bones. Yes, mother's milk is good. But who says we need the milk of other animals for the rest of our lives? Even the animals do not drink another animal's milk after weaning away from their own mother's milk. Then why do we continue drinking milk? Is it necessary, or are we doing it out of habit and conditioning?

Do you know that the glass of milk on your table is meant for the innocent calf? How would you feel if your child were denied its mother's milk? We never try to relate such problems with the animal kingdom. As though they are meant for human exploitation, we continue abusing them. The milk that we drink comes from the cows and buffaloes that are tortured, tormented, and abused in every way. How can we talk about non-violence (Ahimsa) when there is violence in our living? Isaac Singer, the Nobel peace prize winner once said, *"How can we ask mercy from God if we cannot give mercy to others."* We will only get what we give. If we give joy to others we will get joy but if we give pain, we will only get pain in return.

So let us find out the real story behind the milk industry and learn about the horrifying conditions under which the cows are being milked. The following is an excerpt taken from the book *"Heads And Tails"* by Menaka Gandhi where she explains the fate of cows. This happens in India and also in the other parts of the world where cows are exploited and badly abused.

A continual flow of milk is extracted from the dairy cow only by subjecting her to yearly pregnancies - starting from the age of two and each lasting nine months. After giving birth she will be milked for 10 months - but will be impregnated with semen during her third month and for the remaining seven months she will be milked when pregnant. She has only six to eight weeks between pregnancies. She will be milked twice or more times a day and the average Indian cow used in the Indian milk industry gives five times as much as she would have in the Fifties as she has been genetically bred for bigger and softer udders.

In order to give a higher yield, the cow is fed concentrated pellets of Soya bean and cereal (which could have fed a great many more people). But even then the demanded production of milk outstrips her appetite and she starts breaking down body tissue to produce the milk. The result is an illness called ketosis.

Another illness that she contracts early is rumen acidosis induced by large helpings of quickly fermented carbohydrate, this disease leads to lameness. Most of the day the cow stands tied in a narrow stall in her own excrement and udder infections like mastitis, (a painful inflammation of the udder), step in. This long suffering, sick cow is kept alive by antibiotics, hormones and other drugs - all of which come to you in the morning milk.

Each year, 20 percent of these dairy cows are taken out due to infertility or disease. These are then starved to death or sent by truck to the slaughterhouse to provide beef for those that see nothing wrong in eating it. Milk production is very closely allied to the meat trade. No cow lives out her normal life span. She is milked, made sick and then killed.

What happens to the calf? All the calves are separated from their mothers after three days. If the calf is a healthy female, it is put on milk substitutes to become a dairy replacement in two years. The male calves are tied up and left to starve to death, which usually takes a week of intense suffering. Some are stuffed into trucks, one on top of the other, and sent to the slaughterhouse illegally, to be killed for the veal that people eat in restaurants, which is also illegal. Some are sold to the cheese industry to have their stomachs slit (while alive) for rennet, the acid that is extracted for cheese making. A few are selected as bulls and kept in solitary pens for the rest of their lives for artificial insemination. Sometimes, when they are old, they are left on the streets of a city, to wander around till a truck hits them (I should know: In one week, I have picked up eight dying bulls).

What is the basic nature of a cow? To devotedly care for her young, quietly forage and ruminate and patiently live out her 20 odd years in harmony with nature. She is not a four-legged milk pump who is to be orphaned, bred, fed, medicated, inseminated and manipulated for a single purpose - maximum milk at minimum cost.

Have you seen the aged old Indian dairy custom phookan - which is illegal by law but which is practiced on thousands of cows daily? As soon as the cow's milk starts getting less, a stick is poked into her uterus and manipulated causing her intense pain in the belief that this stress will lead to a gush of more milk in the udder. This custom causes sores in the uterus - think about it, women - but what does it matter when the cow is at the end of her milk-giving life anyway and, due to be either tied up and starved or to be thrown into a truck with 40 others and taken to the butcher?

There is this belief that dairy products give a lot of protein and iron. Most people who consume a lot of milk, specially vegetarians, in North India the people who believe that milk and paneer are a protein substitute for meat, have been found to have an iron deficiency causing anemia. Milk not only provides no iron - it actually blocks its absorption. Vegetables are the best source of iron. For instance, 50 gallons of milk are the equivalent (in iron content) of one bowl of spinach.

But what is the point of eating green vegetables if your single glass of milk is going to prevent the absorption of iron that you get from them? Listen to your body. Have you noticed that when you fall even slightly sick, the body feels nauseated at the thought of milk, that doctors recommend that you give it up till your are well? That is because after the age of four a large percentage of people lose the ability to digest lactose, the carbohydrate found in milk. The results often are in symptoms of persistent diarrhea, gas and stomach cramps. (As far as protein is concerned, milk gives the same amount as most vegetables and less than some vegetables). A human being's total protein requirement is 4-5 percent of this daily calorific intake. Nature has arranged her food in such a manner that even if you live on a diet of chappati and potatoes, you will still get more than that amount!

The alternative to dairy products is Soya milk that contains vitamins and tastes as good (or bad). It makes excellent dahi, paneer, ice cream, butter, cheese and milk chocolate, vegetable margarine and plain calcium tablets - which cost much less than milk.

Milk is an unnecessary theft. Do you think that a calf would benefit from your mother's milk? No, it wouldn't. So how will you benefit from its mother's milk? Most of Southeast Asia and the Middle East don't touch the stuff and rightly so. All studies have shown that Asians have the highest intolerance to lactose. In India we have been sold the idea by concentrated western advertising over the last so many years. *"Nature's most perfect food"* is far from that - it is the equivalent of a placebo, and a dangerous one! And, more importantly, apart from harming yourself, every glass of milk that you drink, every ice cream, every pat of butter, ensures that enormous cruelty to a gentle animal and its offspring goes on.

Here it seems appropriate to mention one thing more and that is the ignorant practices of using milk and it's by-products in the temple ceremonies and rituals. The practices of bathing the statues (abhishek) with milk, offering sweets to the Gods made of milk as part of the rituals have creeped in the temple, polluting the very sanctity of the place and the environment. It is a violent waste to let all this milk go down the drain where it becomes the breeding place of ants and bacteria. These kinds of practices must stop and the original way of bathing (abhishek) with clean and pure water should be maintained.

Most private breeders will not sell dogs to pet shops because the care the animals receive is often little better than the conditions in puppy mills. Dogs kept in small cages without exercise, love, or human contact develop undesirable behaviors and may become destructive or unsociable or bark excessively. Also, unlike humane societies and shelters, most pet shops do not inspect the future homes of the dogs they sell. They also dispose of unsold animals in whatever manner they see fit, and allegations of cruel killing methods abound. Poor enforcement of humane laws allows badly run pet shops to continue selling sick, unfit animals, although humane societies and police departments sometimes succeed in closing down pet shops where severe abuse is uncovered.

Pramoda Chitrabhanu
Jain Meditation International Center, New York

Alternatives to Animal Abuse

The information in this article will help you minimize the daily suffering and exploitation of living creatures. Most people increase their intake of eggs and milk when they start a vegetarian diet. Many vegetarians do not realize the gross exploitation involved in supporting the dairy industry, as well as the wool, leather goods and fur industries. Here are some of the facts and alternatives for you to consider.

Facts About Violence

Factory Farming is the method of intensive breeding used today which employs high production assembly line technology and reduces mammals and birds to production units confined under the most inhumane conditions. Stress, disease, pain and suffering for the animals are the inevitable results.

Ethics of Ahimsa (Non - violence)

Cows

The cow, a naturally docile animal, has been turned into a flesh and milk machine, drugged and injected with hormones and antibiotics. She ultimately suffers the horrors of the slaughterhouse when she is no longer profitable as a producer of milk and veal.

Cows are artificially forced into a continuous state of pregnancy and made to produce 400 times their normal amount of milk. This results in widespread infectious diseases unknown to them under natural conditions and necessitates the use of various antibiotics.

Newborn calves are taken from their mothers so that we can drink the milk intended for them. They are placed in dark wooden crates, fed an anemia inducing liquid diet, all to produce white veal.

Rennet, used to curdle most cheeses, is obtained from the stomach of a freshly killed very young calf.

Chickens

Factory farm bred layer hens are confined 4 to 5 per 1 to 2 square feet wire mesh cages arranged in tiers. Over 90% of all eggs produced come from factory farms.

A broiler chicken's life is around 8 to10 weeks. The average space allotted them is about 1/2 square foot per bird.

This overcrowding produces such stress and neurotic behavior in the birds that they resort to feather-pecking, scratching and cannibalism. The solution to this is to clip half of the upper and lower beaks of all the birds by putting them through a hot knife machine, to clip their toes, to keep them in constant dim lighting and feed them anti-stress chemicals added to their water and food.

"Free-range" hens are ultimately slaughtered when their productivity drops off.

Sheep

Sheep by nature, do not have "too much" wool. Scientific breeding, under factory farm conditions, creates an excessive amount of wool.

Sheep are shorn continuously in all seasons. Every year, hundreds of thousands of sheep die from exposure to cold. A closely shorn sheep is more sensitive to cold than a naked human.

Sheep are not shorn by "experts" as we see in educational films. The truth is that sheep are pinned down violently and shorn quickly while blood-staunchers stand by to cover the cuts with tar.

Old sheep are ultimately shipped to the slaughterhouse in abominable conditions and without food or water.

If people were to stop eating lamb and mutton, sheep would still be raised for their wool alone. Buying woolen products supports this cruelty.

Bees

Bees are bred commercially. Their honey and combs are taken from them, and they are given a cheap sugar substitute on which they cannot survive. Thousands upon thousands of bees die. Honey also contains natural toxins which act as a preservative and are harmful to humans.

Fur-Bearing Animals

Most often, the trapping of fur-bearing animals does not result in a quick death. The most commonly used traps are the steel leghold. The trapped animals often are caught for days until the traps are checked. Many chew their own limbs-off to escape. Trapping results not only in painful anguish for the trapped animal, but also starvation for its young.

Commercially bred, fur-bearing animals (such as mink) are raised in cramped anxiety-provoking pens and do not live to reach one year. The methods of killing them are painful, in order to avoid scarring the valuable coats.

Cosmetics and Animal testing

Cosmetics include toothpaste, shampoo, mouthwash, talcum, hand lotions, lipsticks, eye cosmetics, face creams, hair conditioners, perfumes and colognes. Most cosmetics contain animal products and are tested on animals in laboratories. Though the FDA does not require such testing, they endorse the Gillette procedures for tests on animals.

Common tests on animals are the LD/50 test which induces death in 50% of the animals used (rats, mice, guinea pigs and dogs) to determine the lethal dose of a product; the Draize test, used to measure eye irritancy in cosmetics and other products by restraining rabbits and administering increasing amounts of the product directly to the cornea; the Acute Dermal Toxicity test which presses the substance on the shaved skin of an animal after abrasions have been made on its skin and there are still other tests done on animals.

Soaps usually contain animal fats like tallow (stearic acid and related salts). Shampoos can contain tallow, animal glycerin, placenta collagen, animal proteins, and fish liver oil. Many commercial toothpaste contain animal glycerin.

Expensive perfumes commonly contain musk, a secretion scraped from the genitals of male civet cats in Ethiopia. These cats undergo hundreds of such painful scrapings during their lifetime.

Use of Animals in Entertainment

Circuses, Zoos, Rodeos, Horse Racing, etc. Animals, for the most part, are put through painful training and forced to perform, totally alien to their natural way of life. The living condition is also unnatural. Countless animals are killed before a good specimen is captured to fill the many zoos and circuses. Many animals die in transport. Their young ones are left behind to starve. Electric prods are used in rodeos, and the gentle domesticated steers and horses are made to "buck" by a leather belt tightened around their abdomens pressing against their genitals. Horns are broken, animals are strangled while being roped, kicked and abused. Circus animals are forced to perform as freaks. The training is very unpleasant. Horses bred for racing are genetically bred by humans for swiftness, but suffer constantly from weak and sprained ankles, broken bones and drug abuse. Often, they must be "destroyed".

Impact on Health

Meat, cheese and eggs are extremely high in saturated fats and the cholesterol that accumulates on the arterial walls is the major factor of heart attacks.

Large amounts of antibiotics and chemicals are readily used to control the vast amounts of diseases those meat animals, cows, and chickens are prone to get due to their unnatural living and breeding conditions. The drugs are present in the animals' meat, milk and eggs.

The kidneys of a moderate meat eater work three times harder than that of a vegetarian. This is due to the excess toxic wastes in meat, which the kidneys try to eliminate.

Lard, the white rendered fat of a hog is not readily digestible. It is used widely in commercially baked goods and many name brand products.

Less radioactive fallout is found In vegetable milks (cows milk generally shows a count of 98 of the element Strontium 90 compared to a count of 2.1 in vegetable-based milk).

Cow's milk has a different constitution from human's milk. Cow's milk is made of elements that help in developing animal, whereas human milk helps build the nerves and brain faster than the bulk of the body.

Cow's milk is not the only source of calcium. Its content in cow's milk is 120 mg. per 100 grams; Brazil nuts have 176-186 mg.; almonds have 234-247 mg.; kale has 179-200 mg.; sea kelp has over 1,000 mg.; and unhulled sesame seeds have 1, 160 mg.; just to name a few other sources.

Impact on Economics, Ecology and Environment

The waste and fecal matter, chemicals, grease etc. from the meat packing industry empties into our sewer systems and then into our rivers. Slaughterhouses and feedlots are some of the worst polluters of land, water and air. A diet including meat and dairy products requires the daily consumption of 8 times more gallons of water than that needed to produce non-animal foods. Non-animal diets require 1/4 acre per person, whereas meat and dairy eaters require over 2 acres.

One half of the world's population is hungry or malnourished. There is a shortage of over 8 million tons of food, rising to an estimated 100 million tons by the year 2000. A total-vegetarian diet would END the world hunger crisis.

Alternatives
Food Alternatives

Animal Protein

Beans and legumes (lentils), whole grains, nuts, tofu, avocado, olives, hummus, "Good Tasting Nutritional Yeastö" by the farm, vegetable protein such as processed vegetable foods in health food stores such as protose, Big Franks and Loma Linda Sandwich Spread.

Legume + Grain, Legume + Seed, or Legume + Nut combinations result in high quality complete proteins (rice + beans, lentils + rice, beans + corn).

Milk

Commercially prepared vegetable milk such as soymilk (in health food stores). Nut milks may be made at home in a blender in many varieties and delicious flavors. Fruits and vegetable juices are also a substitute for milk.

Eggs

In baking, use an egg replacement. With satisfactory results, you may leave eggs out of many recipes that call for them.

Calcium

Almonds, Sesame seeds, Tahini, dark green leafy vegetables, corn, molasses, seaweed, dried figs, sunflower seeds.

Iron

Dried fruits such as raisins and figs, dark green leafy vegetables, molasses, seaweed (kelp) black walnuts, almonds, and cashews.

Butter Soya margarine such as "Willow Run" and "Hains" contain no animal products; in health food stores as well as regular super markets.

Cheese

Tofu, or soybean cheese or curd maybe used in many ways as a cheese replacement.

Honey

Maple syrup, blackstrap molasses, date sugar.

Clothing Alternatives

Wool

Acrylic, rayon, Orion (for sweaters, blankets etc.).

Leather

Non-leather shoes, belt, purses, wallets, etc.

Silk

Acetate, nylon, satin.

Fur

Use "Fake" Furs made of acrylics.

Toiletries Alternatives :

Use toiletries without lanolin, animal glycerin, tallow or any other animal product. Generally, all commercially prepared soaps contain tallow or animal fats. If you can't determine ingredients from the labels, AVOID and write the manufacturer for more information.

Household Goods Alternatives:

Pillows

Use Acrylic non-allergic material.

Blankets

Use Acrylic, nylon material.

Rugs & Carpets

Use Acrylic, nylon, cottons.

Mattresses & Furniture

Avoid horsehair and other animal hairs.

Brushes

Avoid "natural bristlesö - they come from boars. Use nylon only.

Greases and Polishes

If labels don't have all ingredients, check out your favorite products by writing to the manufacturer.

Medicines, Drugs, Vitamins Alternatives:

Vaccines, Serums, many Drugs and vitamins contain either animal products or were tested on animals. Meditation and yoga along with a good balanced diet, fresh air, enough water and rest diminish the need for frequent drug remedies. Occasional fasting and some herbs are some natural remedies.

Sports, Entertainment Alternatives:

Encourage humane alternatives to hunting, racing, fishing, zoos, rodeos, and circuses, such as educational films of animals in their natural habitats, books and other educational materials.

Animal Based Additives to Avoid :

Calcium Stearates

Stearates most often refer to a fatty substance taken from the stomachs of pigs. It acts as an emulsifier, also found in the form of sodium sterile lactylate and stearic acid.

Lactic Acid

A byproduct of the slaughter-house.

Red Dye, Cochineal

70,000 beetles are killed to produce one pound.

Rennet

Rennet is an enzyme taken from the stomachs of very young calves and is used in clotting milk to make most cheeses. Friendship Cotage has none.

Gelatin

Dried protein extracted from the bones, tendons and skins of animasl.

Lipase

An enzyme from the stomachs and tongue glands of calves, kids and lambs.

Glycerol Monostearate

Glycerol Monostearate is used as an emulsifier. It is hydrolyzed protein often of animal origin.

Pepsin

a clotting agent derived from pigs, which is used in some cheese and vitamins.

Sperm Oil

Hydrogenated whalc oil used in much margarine, but mainly for cosmetics and toiletries as well as in the leather industry.

Stearic Acid

Stearic Acid comes from the slaughterhouse and is a product of pigs used in making soaps.

Vitamin D2 & D3

Vitamin D2 & D3 may be from fish oil, often in milk.

It is a good idea to write the manufacturer when in doubt of a product. Please share with others the information you may have about animal substances especially in food products.

What Our Readers Say:
About My Visit to a Dairy Farm

Subject: Thank you for opening my eyes
Date: Fri, 5 Sep 1997 12:40:23 -1000
From: "h2oMan" <gurrez@aloha.net>

Your message brought tears to my eyes. Literally. At one time I too felt that there was no way I would give up the burfies, lassies, halwas, and ghee reeking rice dishes etc. After all what was Indian food without the heavenly aroma of satvic ghee? And did not our saints use them? At the same time I knew I was but a liar, and worst, to my own self. Only on making a commitment to a vegan diet and life-style could I find peace. Knowing that cows and other animals suffer as they do on the animal farms, it is not possible to use them or their excretions as guilt free nurture. And now I learn that even in India we are subjecting the cows to the tortures of dairy technology!

You cannot know what inspiration you have given me to hear another Indian take the vegan view on butter, milk, etc. I am saving your post to show others and to use in times I may find myself making excuses.

G

Date: Thu, 20 Aug 1998 12:11:05 -0700
From: "Baid, Jyoti" <Jyoti_Baid@affymetrix.com>

That was a very complete and well-written article on the dairy industry in USA. Even after having read numerous articles on the subject its left me extremely disturbed.

I've been almost vegan for over 2 years now, since I first heard this horror story. My husband is gradually converting and our son is born with dairy allergy............

Jyoti Baid

Date: Mon, 29 Sep 1997 09:15:46 +0500
From: Sailu <sl_comdc@sriven.scs.co.in>

Moods are off after I gone through your mail. Actually I have seen your mail two days back. In these two days whenever I take a sip of Tea I am just getting all that matter what you've written. It is really paining to digest the facts. ....

Sailu.

Date: Tue, 23 Sep 1997 00:32:55 -0400 (EDT)
From: APati@aol.com

Many thanks for sharing your tour of the dairy. My stomach curdled with dismay. I am an imperfect vegan. I heard Howard Lyman's speech and a woman animal life right activist came to me in a dream. My father, from Orissa had a heart attack from a meat-centered diet. He is a semi-veg now, and has returned to the plant-based diet of his ancestral past. Your account was moving and I thank you. I will be sharing it, a lot!

Anita Pati @ AOL.com

Date: 25 Aug 98 11:59:27 -0700
From: RAMARNAT@us.oracle.com>

Your article was very nice. **I don't belong to the Jain community but I am a Tamil vegetarian trying to become a vegan and I am all for non-violence.** We have a bunch of animals (dogs, cats, cows, goats.., rats (?)) at home and we try to be as nice as possible to these creatures. I could make sense out of every word you had written.

Amar

Date: Thu, 04 Sep 1997 12:13:29 -0700
From: Janak Lalan <jlalan@pacbell.net>

I am thankful to Mr. Pravin Shah for giving such information. I am sure very soon you will realize that you have done very great thing. You are real 'Jain'.

Bina Lalan.

Date: Mon, 08 Sep 1997 16:38:50 -0700
From: Deepak Patel <pateld@BayNetworks.COM>

I like your mail very much. I know that it's not a question of liking or disliking, **it's horrible fact.** I am vegi ....

Deepak Patel - Bay Networks Inc.

Date: Wed, 19 Aug 1998 08:33:28 -0700 (PDT)
From: Frank Riela <friela@conflictnet.org>

Your note affirmed in me all the reasons I have been vegan for several years now. Although disturbing to read these things, it's good to be reminded of why we live a certain way. What I mean is ... being vegan has simply been for me ... the way I eat.

Also, all my blood work continues to be excellent. Low cholesterol, good iron levels, etc. Since I've been vegan my weight is naturally maintained at the right level and I feel healthy, both physically and in spirit.

Frank Riela

Date: Sun, 2 Nov 1997 08:28:43 -0500
From:"Ian R.Duncan"

I greatly appreciated your bringing to the jainlist the subject of the dairy industry, even though it would have caused a lot of anxiety among some readers.

There is of course a flourishing vegan tradition in "the west", including the USA, based on health & moral considerations rather than exclusively religious ones,

http://hacres.com/html/cannibal.html

Ian Duncan,   Rome, Italy

Date: Thu, 20 Aug 1998 10:48:15 -0400
From: Joanne Stepaniak <joanne@vegsource.org>

I was forwarded your article "My Visit to a Dairy Farm" and would like to thank you for all that you are doing to bring vegan awareness to the Jain community. **Although I am not Jain, I support the philosophy and ethics behind the Jain way of life.**

I am the author of several vegan cookbooks including "The Uncheese Cookbook" and "Vegan Vittles," among others. In my books I reiterate the plight of the dairy cow, as it is such an overlooked and vitally important issue. ....

It is wonderful that you made the commitment to become vegan when you were "older." You are a beautiful example for all — young and old — who might feel it is too difficult to change. I wish you the best with your endeavors. You are doing very valuable and important work.

Joanne Stepaniak - Joanne@vegsource.org

http://www.vegsource.org/joanne

Date: Mon, 24 Aug 1998 09:36:19 -0400 (EDT)
From: "K. R. Shah" <kshah@math.uwaterloo.ca>

I wanted to add that we recently had a wedding reception for our son Nikhil in Bombay, India where the menu was entirely vegan and no one noticed! We received very many complements regarding the delicious food items.

Kirti R. shah - Toronto, Canada

Date: Mon, 22 Sep 1997 09:15:53 -0500
From: Mona shah <Monica.M.Shah-1@tc.umn.edu>

I have read your article "my visit to a dairy farm" and liked the personal perspective you gave.

I am already vegan in diet and try to be in other materials as well like clothes etc. **I feel that the biggest thing left to change for me is reducing or eliminating use of animal products in Jain rituals**. My parents and our Jain center still incorporate animal products in these rituals.

Mona Shah

Date: Wed, 02 Sep 1998 12:50:47 EDT
From: "Kingcross Beach" <kingcross@hotmail.com>

Thanks for the e-mail with valuable information. **I am ashamed to realize how ignorant I am.** I will also share this information with my friends.

N. Ravi

Date: Mon, 24 Aug 1998 12:25:57 PDT
From: "PARIND SHAH" <parind@hotmail.com>

I read your article on COW'S MILK through e-mail sent by one of my respected uncle here. I came here 1.5 years back, since then I try not to eat KANDMUL and so far I'm successful in doing so most of the times But I do use milk and its products.....I'm terrified by the facts I read. Can you please explain how you avoid milk and its products in every day life?

Parind Shah

Date: Mon, 24 Aug 1998 21:33:14 EDT
From: hkmehta1@juno.com (Haresh Mehta)

My name is Riddhi Mehta and I am 16 years old and I just moved to Boston, MA from Columbia, SC.   I was deeply hurt by the info you gave me, not your opinion, but the story and the manslaughter. In May of 97', I stopped eating eggs and cheese (because of rennet) because of a lecture that Guru Chitrabhanuji gave in Columbia.

I thank you for informing me on what was oblivious to me.

Riddhi

Date: Tue, 21 Apr 1998 18:25:27 EDT
From: Instyplano <Instyplano@aol.com>

Jai Jinendra! My name is Atul Khara. I am here in Dallas, Texas, past President and current Board Member of the Jain Society of North Texas.

First of all, thanks for the research and detailed article that was published in JivDaya. I am sure the articulate detail you have provided will help many Jains to decide against using dairy products. One clarification I would like to make is that most of the Digambars do not use milk in the rituals. Also no scriptures supports the use of milk in rituals. Some Digambars in South have started using the milk in their rituals, which is direct influence of Hindu rituals.

Atul.

Appendix - Resource Center

I - Vegetarian Definition

Ovo-lacto vegetarian:

People who do not eat meat of animals such as chicken, pigs, cows, etc. Also they do not eat fish and seafood. But they do eat eggs, egg products, milk and other dairy products. (Some Americans claim that they are vegetarian but they eat chicken and fish, by this definition they are not vegetarian)

Lacto-vegetarian:

People who do not eat meat of animals, eggs, egg products, fish, and seafood. But they do use milk and other dairy products.

Eggitarian:

A lacto-vegetarian, who would not eat eggs explicitly, but will eat cookies, cakes, etc. that may contain eggs.

Vegan:

People who avoid all animal products: meat, fish, seafood, eggs, egg products, milk, cheese, butter, Ghee, Ice cream other dairy products, and honey. In addition, they avoid wearing leather, wool, silk, and use of other animal products.

II - Recommended Reading Material

The Compassionate Cook by Ingrid Newkirk

Favorite recipes from PETA staff and members. Available from PETA (www.peta-online.org).

Cooking with PETA (PETA)

In addition to more than 200 recipes, this book includes helpful information on how and why to become vegetarian. Available from PETA (www.peta-online.org).

Diet for a New America by John Robbins.

Exposes the cruelty, wastefulness, and ecological impact of mechanized meat production. Available from PETA (www.peta-online.org).

Eat More, Weigh Less by Dr. Dean Ornish.

Dr. Dean Ornish's Life Choice Program for Losing Weight Safely Available from PETA (www.peta-online.org).

Eat Right, Live Longer by Neal Barnard, M.D.

Using the Natural Power of Foods to Age-Proof Your Body Available from PCRM (www.pcrm.org) and PETA (www.peta-online.org).

Enemies, A Love Story by I. B. Singer.

This farcical comedy is also a subtle exploration of the parallels between Holocaust refugees and non-human victims of persecution.

Instead of Chicken, Instead of Turkey by Karen Davis.

Features vegan alternatives to poultry and eggs.

The Jungle by Sinclair.

The classic novel that exposed corrupt conditions in the Chicago meatpacking industry.

The McDougall Plan for Super Health (McDougall and McDougall)

An easy to understand explanation of how to "look better, feel better, and stay better."

Slaughterhouse by Eisnitz.

The shocking story of greed, neglect, and inhumane treatment inside the U.S. meat industry.

Vegan: The New Ethics of Eating (Marcus)

A thorough and engaging overview of the health, ecological, and ethical issues surrounding the human diet.

Vegan Nutrition Pure and Simple by Michael Klaper.

Clarifies the consequences of eating animal products and expounding the benefits of a vegan diet.

Additional reading material

1   Don't Drink Your Milk .... Dr. Frank Oski
2   Dr. Dean Ornish's Program for
    Reversing Heart Disease .... Dr. Dean Ornish
3   Pregnancy, Children, and the Vegan Diet .... Dr. Michael Klaper
4   Reclaiming Our Health .... John Robbins
5   Diet for a New America the Video .... John Robbins
6   A Physician's Slimming Guide for
    Permanent Weight Control .... Dr. Neal Barnard
7   Food for Life .... Dr. Neal Barnard
8   Foods That Cause You Lose Weight .... Dr. Neal Barnard
9   The Power of Your Plate .... Dr. Neal Barnard
10 Milk, A Message to My Patients .... Dr. Robert Kradjian
11 Save Yourself from Breast Cancer .... Dr. Robert Kradjian
12 Get the Fat Out .... Victoria Moran
13 Compassion: The Ultimate Ethic .... Victoria Moran
14 The Love Powered Diet .... Victoria Moran
15 Why Be a Vegetarian? .... Sheth
16 Quit for Good .... Ralph C. Cinque
17 Food Allergies Made Simple .... Phyllis Austin and
                                                                          Drs. Agatha & Calvin Thrash
18 Carpal Tunnel Syndrome (Prevention,
    Treatment, Recovery) .... Orthodox Views
19 The Tofu Toll Booth .... Dar Williams
20 Let There be Light .... Darius Dinshah
21 Conscious Eating .... Dr. Gabriel Cousins
22 The Science and Fine Art of Natural Hygiene .... Dr. Herbert M. Sheldon
23 Natural Hygience (The Pristine Way of Life) ...... Dr. Herbert M. Sheldon
24 Fasting and Eating for Health .... Dr. Joel Fuhman
25 Medical Drugs on Trial: Verdict Guilty .... Dr. K.R. Sidhwa
26 A Race for Life (From Cancer to Ironman) .... Dr. Ruth Heidrich
27 Health for All .... Dr. Shelton
28 First Aid, the Natural Way .... Dr. Sidhwa
29 Diabetes and Hypoglycemic Syndrome .... Drs. Agatha & Calvin Thrash
30 Long Life Now (Strategies for Staying Alive) ...... Lee Hitchcox

Many of the above books are commonly available at most health and natural food stores, and many vegetarian societies also stock them. The easiest way to buy them is by mail-order from:

American Vegan Society, P.O. Box H, Malaga, NJ 08328.

III - List of Organizations of Animal care and Non-violent Activities:

People for the Ethical Treatment of Animals (PETA)

757-622-PETA (7382), fax: 757-622-0457
501 Front St., Norfolk, VA 23510
Web Site: www.peta-online.org,
e-mail: peta@norfolk.infi.net

Exposes animal abuse and promotes respect for animals. Its credo is, "Animals are not ours to eat, wear, experiment on, or use for entertainment." PETA is probably the largest organization of its kind, now has global presence in many countries.

Physicians Committee for Responsible Medicine (PCRM)

202-686-2210, fax: 202-686-2216,
P.O. Box 6322, Washington, DC 20015
Web site: www.pcrm.org,
e-mail: pcrm@pcrm.org

Comprised of physicians and lay members; promotes nutrition, preventive medicine, and ethical research practices; publishers of *Good Medicine* magazine. PCRM is all pro-animals! Not only they stand for strictly vegetarian diets, but also against using animals in laboratories. They lobby hard in the Congress for eliminating meat and dairy from food pyramid, which is taught in schools and used as a guideline for serving lunches.

Vegetarian Resource Group

410-366-8343, fax: 410-366-8804
P.O. Box 1463, Baltimore, MD 21203
Web site: www.vrg.org

Dedicated to health, ecology, ethics, and world hunger education; produces and sells books and pamphlets. One also finds vegetarian and vegan recipes, vegetarian and vegan nutrition information, vegetarian and vegan cookbooks, Vegetarian Journal excerpts, vegetarian travel information, vegetarian and vegan brochures, and even a Vegetarian Game. Their travel guide for restaurants at http://www.veg.org/veg/Guide/USA/ most useful.

Beauty Without Cruelty - India

Web site: www.bwcindia.org

The organization in India, Beauty Without Cruelty, strives to educate the people about various aspects of living a cruelty-free lifestyle. They define it as "A way of life which causes no creature of land, sea, or air, terror, torture or death."

American Vegan Society

609-694-2887
P.O. Box H, Malaga, NJ 08328

Has an extensive list of available vegetarian books and sponsors annual conferences; oldest American vegetarian organization.

Vegan Outreach

10410 Forbes Rd., Pittsburgh, PA 15235
Web site: www.veganoutreach.org

Distributes the informative booklet, *Why Vegan?*

EarthSave

502-589-7676
600 Distillery Commons, Suite. 200, Louisville, KY 40206
Web site: www.earthsave.org,
e-mail: earthsave@aol.com

An organization committed to environmental and health education; provides materials and support for people who are becoming vegetarian.

Vegan Action

510-654-6297 • P.O. Box 4353, Berkeley, CA 94704-0353
Web site: www.vegan.org

Distributes information on vegan diets and lifestyles and campaigns for the increased availability of vegan foods.

North American Vegetarian Society

518-568-7970 • P.O. Box 72, Dolgeville, NY 13329
Web site: www.cyberveg.org/navs, - www.navs-online.org,
e-mail: navs@telenet.net

Dedicated to the promotion of vegetarianism through education, publications, and annual conferences.

Humane Farming Association

415-771-2253

1550 California St., Suite 6, San Francisco, CA 94109

Leads a national campaign to stop factory farms from misusing chemicals, abusing farm animals, and misleading the public.

Farm Sanctuary

530-865-4617 fax: 530-865-4622
3100 Aikens Rd., Watkins Glen, NY 14891

Works to prevent the abuses in animal farming through legislation, investigative campaigns, education, and direct rescue programs. Operates shelters for rescued farm animals.

Jewish Vegetarians of North America

410-754-5550 • 6938 Reliance Rd., Federalsburg, MD 21632
e-mail: imossman@skipjack.bluecrab.org
Web - www.orbyss.com/jvna.htm

Indian American Dietetic Association (IADA)

Rita (Shah) Batheja, MS RD CDN
Founder, Indian American Dietetic Association
825 Van Buren Street, Baldwin Harbor, NY 11510, USA
Tel: 516-868-0605
E-mail: krbat1@juno.com

American Dietetic Association (ADA)

ADA's Consumer Nutrition Hotline
Tel: 1-800-366-1655   9am - 4pm Central time
Web: www.eatright.org/catalog

Plenty International

P.O. Box 394, Summertown, TN USA 38483
Web site: www.plenty.org,
e-mail: plenty1@usit.net

Has worked with villages around the world since 1979 to enhance nutrition and local food self-sufficiency through vegetarianism.

The Animals' Voice

420 East South Temple #240 • Salt Lake City, UT USA 84111
Tel: 801-539-8100
Web: www.animalsvoice.com/

This site contains what used to be a hard-printed a complete magazine on web, all dedicated to, as the name says, "Animal's Voice." Which is one of the oldest magazines.

Here is what used to be a hard-printed a complete magazine on the web, all dedicated to, as the name says, "Animal's Voice." The address is www.animalsvoice.com/home.html to get started on this one of the oldest magazines.

The Ark Trust

P.O. Box 8191, Universal City, CA, USA 91618-8191
Phone (818) 501-2ARK (2275), Fax (818) 501-2226
Web: www.arktrust.org   E-mail: genesis@arktrust.org

An organization, honoring Hollywood and multi medica celebrities and authors presenting pro-animal issues. www.arktrust.org/ Their motto is, "Cruelty Cannot Stand Spotlight." Their annual Genesis Awards are televised on Animal Planet Channel.

Envirolink Network

Here is a catch-all for all the other sites that you may want to search for: http://envirolink.netforchange.com/ provides a huge list of linkages in various areas of environmental issues, including the ones listed above.

WEBSITES

1	People for the Ethical Treatment of Animals (PETA)	www.peta-online.org
2	Physicians Committee for Responsible Medicine (PCRM)	www.pcrm.org
3	Vegetarian Resource Group	www.vrg.org
4	Beauty Without Cruelty - India	www.bwcindia.org
5	North American Vegan Society	www.cyberveg.org/navs
6	Vegan Outreach	www.veganoutreach.org
7	EarthSave	www.earthsave.org
8	Vegan Action	www.vegan.org
9	North American Vegetarian Society	www.cyberveg.org/navs
10	Humane Farming Association	www.hfa.org/
11	Farm Sanctuary	www.farmsanctuary.org/
12	Jewish Vegetarians of North America	www.orbyss.com/jvna.htm
13	Plenty International	www.plenty.org
14	Animal's Voice	www.animalsvoice.com/
15	The Ark Trust Inc.	www.arktrust.org/
16	EnviroLink Network	http://envirolink.netforchange.com/
17	PETA for India	www.petaindia.org
18	The Animal Law Project	www.animal-law.org
19	Veggie Pets:	www.meatstinks.com/lpals.html
20	Animal Health, Well-being, and Rights	www.tiac.net/users/sbr/animals.html
21	Animals' Agenda	www.animalsagenda.org
22	Jainism and Animal Issues	www.yja.org/jivdaya
23	Charity Birds Hospital	www.exciteasia.com/birds.htm
24	Animal Rights Resource Site. Raising Healthy Vegetarian Dogs and Cats	http://arrs.envirolink.org
25	Ahimsa of Texas – Animal sanctuary (Ratilal and Bonny Shah)	www.ahimsatx.org
26	Shri Mandal Mahajan Panjarapol	www.spaceclub.com/panjarapol/index.html
27	Vegetarian/Vegan Resource	www.vegsource.org
28	The International Vegetarian Union	www.ivu.org
29	Tofutti(tm) Brand Non-Dairy Food Products	www.koshermall.com/tofutti/index.html
30	How to Become a Fruitarian	www.islandnet.com/~arton/fruit.html
31	Vegetarian Society of the UK	www.vegsoc.org
32	Toronto Vegetarian Association	www.veg.on.ca

33	Young Indian Vegetarians of the UK	www.indian-vegetarians.org
34	Vegie World (useful guidance on renewable energy and organic agriculture.)	www.ozemail.com.au/~vego
35	Veggie Shoes	www.vegetarian-shoes.co.uk
36	Vegan Wares Shoe Company	www.veganwares.com
37	Vegetarian Books for Children	http://gate.cruzio.com/~cns/veg
38	The Vegetarian Youth Network	www.geocities.com/rainforest/vines/4482/
39	Teen Vegetarian	www.geocities.com/hotsprings/2657
40	Just for Youth	www.vegsoc.org/youth
41	Towards Freedom. Young Indian Americans Reflect. Led by Sangeeta Kumar of San Diego	www.towardsfreedom.com
42	The Ahimsa Coffeehouse	www.ahimsa.net/vegetarian
43	Vegetarian Pages	www.veg.org/veg
44	101 Reasons	www.geocities.com/rainforest/2062/101.html
45	Alternative Therapies and Vegetarian Diets	www.nursing.upenn.edu/nutritionsitesalt.htm
46	Vegetarianism in World Religions	www.vsc.org/page41.html
47	All-Creatures: A Biblical Supersite	www.all-creatures.org
48	Vegetarianism & Islamic Thought	www.islamveg.com
49	Islamic Vegetarian Recipes	www.veg.on.ca/newsletr/janfeb96 islam_recipes.html
50	Buddhism and Biotechnology	http://online.sfsu.edu/~rone/
51	Sister Clara Muhammad's VegetarianCookery ourfamily	www.seventhfam.com/scmhwc vegetarian.htm

Excerpts from Environmental News
Recycling department of IBM, Raleigh, NC
October 20, 1998

Excerpts:
How our Diet affects the Environment

We don't think anyone should tell us what to eat - that's too personal. But we do think you should know some facts about how your diet affects the environment.

- Believe it or not, cows may be contributing to the greenhouse effect. According to one estimate, the world's 1.3 billion cows annually produce nearly 100 million tons of methane - a powerful greenhouse gas that, molecule for molecule, traps 25 times as much solar heat as CO2.

- Livestock (Cattle, Calves, Hogs, Pigs etc) production accounts for more than half of all the water consumed (for all purposes) in the USA.

- A third of the surface of North America is devoted to grazing. Half of American croplands grow livestock feed (mostly for cattle) for meat and dairy products.

- 220 million acres of land in the USA have been deforested for livestock production.

- 25 million acres (an area the size of Austria) in Brazil, and half the forests in Central America, have been cleared for beef production.

- The value of raw materials consumed to produce food from livestock is greater than the value of all oil, gas and coal consumed in America.

- Growing grains, vegetables and fruits uses less than 5% as much raw materials as does meat and dairy production.

According to *DIET FOR A NEW AMERICA:* If Americans reduced their meat intake by just 10%, the savings in grains and soybeans could adequately feed 60 million people - the number of people who starve to death, worldwide, each year.

Notes

Notes

Notes